America -
The Architect of
My Destiny

Tatiana Potinga Merry

ISBN 978-0-578-28270-1

Copyright © 2022 by Tatiana Potinga Merry

All rights reserved, including the right of reproduction in any form, or by any mechanical or electronic means including photocopying or recording, or by any information storage or retrieval system, in whole or in part in any form, and in any case not without the written permission of the author and publisher.

Many thanks to Hoagie Merry and Kelsey Steele for their contributions.

Published July 2022

Dedication

For my parents, Andrei and Vera Potinga.
From whose stoic perspectives on life and value of it,
I inherited; and, whose honor of our Lord,
Jesus Christ, I affirm.

Foreword

What inspired the writing of this book.

Accepting the challenge and acknowledging God.

Understanding that no matter your standing,
you are the author of your own destiny.

Value and appreciation for the opportunity
to become an American citizen.

Quote of the Man in the Arena by Theodore Roosevelt.

Contents

Introduction xi

Chapter 1: The Seeds 1
 1. The First Time 1
 2. God's Plan 3
 3. The Grandparents 4
 4. The Parents 11
 5. Post-Traumatic Growth Syndrome 16
 6. The Land of Everyone and No One 19
 7. The Land of Wine 23
 8. No Materialism, Just Love 26
 9. Early School Years 30
 10. The Iron Curtain 33

Chapter 2: The Roots 37
 1. America Through A Soviet Lens 37
 2. There's No Clean Breakup 40
 3. Vodka In The Attic 42
 4. The Duck and Vacuum 45
 5. The Vision 47
 6. Higher Education or Socialism 50
 7. Out of the Frying Pan; Into the Fire 54
 8. The Interview with The Americans 57

Chapter 3: Branching Out 61
1. America, Here I Come 61
2. Housekeeping 63
3. The Opportunity 67
4. Goodbye Moldova 70
5. Welcome Back, Sweetheart! 72
6. The Sweet Beginning 74
7. I Got Wheels 78
8. The Bank on the Corner of the Street 82
9. Free Education 86

Chapter 4: The Fruits of My Labor 89
1. No Success Without Failure 89
2. The Kid in the Candy Store 92
3. Throw your Running Shoes off the Balcony 97
4. Don't Take "No" For An Answer 100
5. The Mentor 105
6. The Divine Intervention 108
7. Becoming An "American" 112

Introduction

Since I can remember, I always knew there was something bigger and better in the world than what I knew. I could not put it into words. It was a feeling I had, an inner voice that was telling me I was destined for something challenging, yet rewarding. Something beyond my imagination. That inner voice was so powerful that it was screaming loud, yet I could not comprehend it. Nothing in the world could silence that voice. No matter how much time has passed that feeling is ever present with me in everything I do and everywhere I go in life. I call that voice the presence of Godly power. The higher spirit. The beginning and the end of everything.

For the last six years I have wanted to write this book. I am not a writer by trade, mind you, and English is my third language, but I love a challenge. In truth, writing in English is my greatest act of vulnerability. Yet, I decided to embrace my vulnerability as my greatest strength. In Brené Brown's words, "Vulnerability is about showing up and being seen. It's tough to do that when we're terrified about what people might see or think." I wanted to write this book to share my stories with other people. People with both similar and different stories. However, I mainly want to share my stories with my family and friends, more so with my kids in the future. This book was inspired by multiple people and events. By hardships, challenges, mistakes, forgiveness, and love.

I am hoping when you read this book you will know that no matter how you see your life, whether it's filled with greatness or flawed with mistakes and heavy burden, no matter who you are, no matter what you were born into, or where you came from, there is a higher place you can reach, one where you can attain greatness. When you read this book, I hope you understand that you are the author of your life story and your life script. If perhaps you don't like your life script, I hope this book helps you realize that you have the ability to rewrite that script; to change it at any time you choose. At the end of every story I include a "lesson learned" message. It's my way of reflecting on what I learned from the experience, because I truly believe that there's something to be learned about ourselves and others in anything we do in our lives.

Before I delve into my stories, I want to start with my favorite quote of all time. This quote, by Theodore Roosevelt, is my everyday motto and relates to me almost to the last word. I even have it framed and hung in our living room so that my husband and I never lose sight of it. This quote was recited by the judge overseeing my U.S. citizenship ceremony, which made me feel sad and proud at the same time. This quote encompasses my thirteen-year journey since I arrived in the United States. Most importantly, this quote inspired and motivated me to write this book:

"It is not the critic who counts; not the man who points out how the strong man stumbles, or where the doer of deeds could have done them better. The credit belongs to the man who is actually in the arena, whose face is marred by dust and sweat and blood; who strives valiantly; who errs, who comes short again and again, because there is no effort without error and shortcoming; but who does actually strive to do the deeds; who knows great enthusiasms, the great devotions; who spends himself in a worthy cause; who at the best knows in the end the triumph of high achievement, and who at the worst, if he fails, at least fails while daring greatly, so that his place shall never be with those cold and timid souls who neither know victory nor defeat."

Chapter 1

THE SEEDS

*"Destiny is no matter of chance.
It is a matter of choice. It is not a thing to be waited
for, it is a thing to be achieved."*
-William Jennings Bryan

The First Time

It was 1994 when, for the first time, I heard about the United States of America. I was in second grade painting class. My teacher, Miss Liz, had laid out several beautiful pictures on the front board. She was describing them with a lot of passion and enthusiasm, as she had traveled there before. Her expressiveness left us mesmerized and intrigued. Out of all the beautiful pictures, one caught my eye. The colors of buff and gray, delicate green and pink, and in its depths, brown, slate-gray, and violet... it was breathtaking. I raised my hand and asked Miss Liz where the place in the picture was. She looked at me and smiled. "This is the Grand Canyon and it is in Arizona, a state located in the United States of America." curiosity immediately gripped me, so I asked another question. "Is it far? Can I get there with my daddy's car?" She smiled once again and said, "it is very far and you can get there only by plane." I looked around at my classmates, then back at my teacher in wonder. I thought to myself, "when I grow up, I will go to America."

Before that day, I never knew about the United States of America, but something intrigued me. Was it the beautiful pictures on the front board? Maybe the vibrant colors or the fact that you could only get there by plane? I did not know the answer. However, I knew it would be an adventure worth taking.

I do not recall whether I went home that day and told my parents about what I'd discovered at school, but I do remember the experience vividly, almost like it was yesterday. Deep in my heart, I knew one day I would visit this wonderful land of opportunities. I remember telling my classmates, with the utmost confidence, that one day I would travel to America. It was never a matter of if, but when. I did not know how a little girl from Ghidighici, Moldova would end up in the greatest country in the world, but I knew I would. That was enough for me to strive, to work hard, and to jump through hoops to make it happen. I was forced to sacrifice the life I had and the family, leaving everything behind, and to believe in my abilities to achieve something great.

Lesson learned: Everything that happens in life has a purpose. If they don't make sense at the moment, they will.

God's Plan

Oftentimes, I think that moment during my second-grade painting class was the moment when God gave me a glimpse of the magnificent journey I was destined to live. God revealed part of the plan he had for my life by putting me in front of that picture of the Grand Canyon. Did I know back then? I do not think so, but my subconscious mind painted a picture for me. I did not know what the future held but I believed God had a plan for me. As a Christian Orthodox, it is one of my deepest beliefs that no event in life occurs without God's divine approval.

I also believe that our destiny is shaped, daily, by our actions and the choices we make. God gives us the freedom of choice; the freedom to be the main character in our story and not a simple participant. It is the collaboration between God's plan and the choices we make along the way that allows us to reach our goals. As the old Romanian proverb says: "God gives it to you, but he doesn't put it in your bag." This suggests that anything obtained by someone in life must be accompanied by effort, hard work, and dedication. You must be ready to recognize and seize any opportunity that presents itself to you.

I believe God's plan and the choices I made brought me to the dream land, the land of opportunity, the amazing United States of America. I know I would have not made it here without God's blessings. God laid the path and I chose to follow it. The path was rocky and filled with plenty of obstacles, but, I would not have preferred it to happen any other way. I understood from an early age that nothing in life comes easy. I watched my parents working day and night to obtain everything they had. There was no easy way to succeed, yet failure was not an option. If you fail, you get up and try again the next day. No regrets, no victimizing; just try again and again until you succeed. To repeat the process requires courage, and courage requires personal sacrifice. The path to success demands you face the risk of failing. I knew I could fail but I did not let the fear of failure throw me off the path. On the contrary, the idea of failure gave me the courage to continue and to not give up. I truly believe this inner force runs through my veins and is embedded in my genes. I have my grandparents and parents to thank for that, which I will share more details about ahead.

Lesson learned: There is always collaboration between God and us humans. He gives you a blessing, but you must be awake to see it and put it to use.

The Grandparents

I was looking over the gate from my grandparents' home into the road and there was Grandpa walking towards me. He was stumbling but trying to walk straight with his chin up. I looked at him and smiled because I knew what was coming next. My favorite time spent with my grandpa was when he told stories. He walked into the house and looked at Grandmother with a serious facial expression that asked, "Do you have anything to say?" My grandmother looked at him, shaking her head without uttering so much as a word. She was sitting in her bed, as she had done for the last six years, due to lower body paralysis.

Grandpa sat on the bed and propped his foot on the chair next to it. He looked at me and said, "help grandpa take his boots off." My face filled with light and happiness. I pulled them off with all my strength and placed them next to the door. He directed a warm smile at me. I sat next to him, knowing that he would begin recounting stories about his time in the war. As he spoke, he maintained a serious demeanor into the abyss. His body was there but his mind was somewhere else. He took a deep breath and said, "my comrades and I were instructed to go to the German camp. When we got there, we proceeded with caution, fearful of a Nazi ambush. But, there was no trace of the German enemy. We spotted some people behind barbed wire. As we approached, it was hard to watch them. I remember their faces, especially their eyes, which portrayed their nightmare." He stopped for a moment, put his head down, and took a deep breath as if he was running out of air. He looked up and continued the stories. "At first, they were scared, but then they realized we were the "good ones" and welcomed us. Their faces lit up with hope and happiness." He stopped again and crossed himself, dropping his chin to his chest. "There were a lot of poor souls. It was a giant hole filled with poor souls, shoes, and hair... oh, God." At this moment, Grandma looked at him and exclaimed, "Stefan, stop with your war stories, you will scare the child! Better give your granddaughter one ruble so she can buy some candies." My grandpa looked at her upset. Grandpa was a thrifty man and Grandma used to prod him on his shoulder to make him take a ruble out of his pocket and give it to me. He did not like that, but he did it because Grandma said so.

My grandfather, Stefan, whom I adored dearly, was a soldier in the Red Army and fought in WWII from beginning to end. He never spoke about the atrocities, death, and pain he experienced during those four years. He only spoke of them after a few drinks. My cousins and I knew that story time was when Grandpa was tipsy. I was the youngest grandchild they had and the one they loved the most. I was always by their side, listening to Grandpa's stories with an open mouth and wide eyes. Back then, I did not comprehend what war was. I only knew it involved a lot of death and pain. The events of the war scarred Grandpa for life, causing him to drink more in order to cope with the stress that came from those memories.

Grandpa was wounded in the right shoulder in 1943 and stayed in the hospital until he was able to fight again. He never gave up, never quit, and fought until the end of the war. What was even worse is the two children my grandparents had before the war all died of hunger. Yes, you read that right: they died of Holodomor, or man-made famine. Holodomor affected the most vulnerable, children and the elderly, first by feeling the effects of malnutrition. The once smiling young faces of children vanished forever amid the constant ache of hunger. It nibbled away at their bellies, which became dreadfully swollen, while their arms and legs resembled sticks as they slowly starved to death. Can you imagine seeing your children's desperation for food while you can't help them? Can you imagine looking at them as they become skin and bones and there is nothing you can do about it? What would that do to you as a mother, a father, or as a human in general? I can't begin to imagine what my grandparents felt, especially my grandmother, who was left alone during the war with their children while my grandfather was sent to the front lines.

This man-made famine was what Stalin, and the Communist Party did to its own people; it is the inevitable outcome of communism and socialism. The Communist Party, under Stalin's leadership, controlled people through fear, starvation, terror, and manipulation. It began with eliminating the intellectual and scholarly pillars of society; this was done to reduce the risk that people would be knowledgeable enough to revolt. They then proceeded to crush the people's spirit. Stalin arrested the remaining scholars and scientists, plus the cultural and religious leaders who were falsely accused of plotting an armed revolt. Those arrested were either executed without a trial or deported to prison camps in remote areas of Russia to be killed, tortured, and forgotten.

Stalin then imposed the Soviet system of land management known as Collectivization. This resulted in the seizure of all privately owned farmlands and livestock, in a country where eighty percent of people were traditional, village farmers. Among those farmers was a class of people who were given the name of "Kulaks" by the Communists. They were formerly wealthy farmers who owned at least twenty-four acres of land or had employed farm workers. Stalin believed any future uprising would be led by these Kulaks, thus he proclaimed a policy aimed at dissolving the Kulaks as a class; both Lenin and Stalin were explicit in this directive. In Stalin's 1929 letter, "Concerning Policy of Liquidating Kulaks As A Class," he expressed, in no uncertain terms, how the Soviet government would approach them: "In order to oust the Kulaks as a class, the resistance of this class must be smashed in open battle and it must be deprived of the productive sources of its existence and development (free use of land, instruments of production, land-renting, right to hire labor, etc.)." (J. V. Stalin Works, Vol. 12 pp. 184-189.)

Next, came the starvation; people could not even think about rebelling against the government because the only thing on their minds was food and hunger. Starvation quickly makes a nation impotent and hopeless. Stalin and the Communist party thought they could do anything they wanted to "the Proletariat," so long as they believed the government was the source of their survival. A famous lesson Stalin gave to his comrades was, "the lesson of the plucked chicken." In 1935, Stalin invited his senior advisors (and some media henchmen) to a meeting with the intent to make a point using the most persuasive of methods. When everyone was gathered at the barnyard, he called for a live chicken and vigorously squeezed it in one hand. With the other, he began plucking out the chicken's feathers in handfuls. The poor bird squawked under the torment, but Stalin kept stripping the chicken until it convulsed with agony. Unmoved by the blatant disgust on the faces of those too afraid to express their unease to the dictator, he continued until the chicken was completely bare. He then put the bird down by a small portion of grain and stood up to finish the final act of his demonstration. While the people curiously observed the chicken move towards the grain and begin to peck, Stalin put his hand into his jacket pocket and pulled out a fistful of grain. Holding it out in front of the wounded bird, to the complete surprise of the hypnotized spectators, the chicken managed a weak-kneed stagger back to Stalin and started to peck the fresh grain right out of his hand; the hand that, moments ago, had inflicted unbearable pain on the creature. Stalin had made his point — loud and clear.

He turned to the audience and said: "People are like this chicken. It doesn't matter how much pain you inflict on them. The moment you offer them what they need, they will still follow you and turn to you for their survival." To me, this demonstration has another, somewhat alternative meaning. It is not despite the pain that Stalin inflicted on the poor bird, but because of it that the bird followed him; and this concept is not exclusive to animals. Our minds become slaves to those we see as having the power to control us and cause us pain. We are quick to give up our autonomy in favor of those who have the power to rule so long as they also hold the keys to our survival. This is the fundamental construct of an oppressed society governed by communist leadership.

Despite the terror and hardship my grandparents lived through, they were the strongest and most courageous people I have ever known. They had twelve kids in total, my father being the last one born. After Grandpa returned from the war, he was a different person; he had a shoulder wound and limp right arm which prevented him from finding a job. Unfortunately, there was no Veterans' Affairs or pensions to provide financial assistance. They were on their own, left to cope with mental disorders such as post-traumatic stress disorder (PTSD), major depressive disorder (MDD), and traumatic brain injury (TBI). No one ever asked my grandfather how he felt, nor did they offer to help him integrate back into society after returning home. He dealt with his trauma as best he could. My grandfather was a highly decorated veteran with multiple medals to his name; my grandmother, likewise, was bequeathed the honorary title of "Mother Heroine." This was the highest rank in the Soviet Union, given to women with many children (ten and up). The title was accompanied by the bestowal of the Order of "Mother Heroine," and a certificate conferred by the Presidium of the Supreme Soviet of the Soviet Union. One would say these are important accomplishments, upon which a lot of respect and admiration is given to its recipients. Unfortunately, this is not the case. After the war was over, the government forgot about my grandparents and their kids; there was not much assistance given to them whatsoever.

I reflect upon this story often. Sometimes because I miss my grandparents, other times because I pass a war memorial. It reminds me of how blessed I am to have the life I currently lead. I can't complain – no, I have no right to complain about anything in my life. I now live in the greatest country; the beacon of light which shines on the rest of the world. In fact, I can't even compare my life to the life my grandparents experienced because it would be ridiculous and shameful to do so. It would be a disgrace to their honor. The only thing I can do is always be thankful for the sacrifices they made, so I could have the wonderful life I have today.

Lesson Learned: Pain doesn't define you, it refines you.

The Parents

My mom and I are in the kitchen cooking Dad's favorite dish. She's in a hurry to make sure everything is ready for Dad's return from Poland where he's been working the past few weeks. Mom makes sure the water is warm for a bath, food is ready, clothes are clean; it feels as if we are getting ready to entertain a very important guest. The guest of honor – our daddy! We celebrated every single time Dad would come home after two weeks abroad. Everyone would be up and ready to welcome our breadwinner. I felt a rush of excitement to know that my father, my hero, was finally coming home. I was definitely daddy's girl! I was full of joy for him to come home because he would always fetch a small gift for his little girl on the way back. My dad was, and still is, my role model. I would stay up late at night, waiting to make sure he got home. We all missed him while he was gone, but we knew the sacrifices he was making was for the benefit of our family. He would arrive home and take a bath, then we would all sit at the table to eat with him. We were so fascinated by the stories during his trips abroad.

I was eleven years old and my brother was fifteen when Dad started his trucking business. The first truck he bought was on credit from a neighbor. The neighbor was a nice person and allowed Dad to work by using the truck before he could pay it off. My dad started his business soon after the Soviet Union collapsed, which were menacing times. The collapse of the Soviet Union created an opportunity for corruption and crime in Moldova, and thus the Moldovan mafia was formed.

These group members ("vor v zakone" aka thief-in-law) were a new generation of recruits, including damaged and disillusioned veterans of the USSR's last war. Some were bodyguards, some were runners, some were leg-breakers and some – some were killers. In the 1990s, everything was up for grabs and the new thief-in-law reached out with both hands. State assets were privatized, businesses forced to pay for protection, and as the iron curtain fell the Russian mafia rolled out into the rest of the world. The thief-in-laws were part of a way of life that, in its own way, mirrored the changes Russia went through in the 20th century. Organized crime truly came into its own in a Moldova that was, itself, becoming more organized. Since the turn of the millennium, the new thief-in-law has adapted again, taking a lower profile or working for the state and government when they must.

In the 90s, small business owners were always in danger of extortion and possible death if they were not "donating" to mafia members or they simply rubbed them the wrong way. Dad had his fair share of encounters with these miscreants. While his business was growing, we received an unwelcome visit from the thief-in-law. My mom and I were home alone while Dad was abroad working. One afternoon, someone knocked on the door; my mom opened it and was greeted by three, intimidating individuals. They had profoundly serious looks on their faces that frightened me as soon as I saw them. One of them barked at my mom, "we are looking for Andrei." She was terrified but her face did not show it. She looked them dead in the eyes and said, "he is at work, what do you need?" The man looked at my mom with a smirk and replied, "we need to speak to him, not you, so when is he coming back?" I could tell Mom was getting frustrated and uncomfortable with their presence, especially with me next to her. She tried to cut the conversation short by proclaiming, "he will be back tomorrow, you can talk to him then." They stepped back from the door and, before turning away, the one man stated, "he knows who we are and where to find us." After closing the door, Mom rushed over to the phone to call Dad. In a small panic, she kept repeating over the phone "vor v zakone" and "krysha." I wasn't sure that those words meant, but I knew those guys were trouble. Dad had to involve my uncle who was a general in the army. He asked for his protection because not even the police could defend him against these criminals. They preyed on hardworking people; defenseless small business owners who earned their money with blood, sweat, and tears. They knew that, by using intimidation and terror tactics, people would give in because there was no other way to get rid of them. However, Dad felt he needed to stop them from terrorizing him and our family; he argued that if he paid them off once, he would have to continue paying in order to keep them from inflicting harm to his business and family. It was a never-ending game.

As you can see, being a small business owner in Moldova after the collapse of the Soviet Union was not easy. On top of having criminals knocking at your door threatening you and your family, you had an unstable government that provided no help to individuals who wanted. For those that were successful in starting a business of their own, there was no assurance that their business would succeed in a country crippled by an economic and monetary market crash; it was the Wild West of Moldova. But, this didn't stop Dad from making sacrifices and working hard to better the life of his family. Oftentimes, he would have conversations with my brother and I, and would say, "I don't want you two to grow up as I did, dealing with poverty and shame. I want a better life for you." These conversations helped me understand what it means to make sacrifices and to strive towards achieving something in life through hard work. I understand why my dad used to feel that way. Not only do I understand my parents on a much deeper level, but I have an enormous amount of respect for them.

I come from a very strong family. A family that does not capitulate in the face of obstacles and doesn't cave when problems knock at the door. A family that fights until there is nothing left to fight for. Another one of these hardships knocked at my parent's door when I was five years old. I had a terrible accident; both of my legs were burned to the bone - 4th degree burns.

Despite multiple surgeries, skin transplants, and six months in the hospital, the doctor's verdict was that I would never walk again; Mom and Dad were devastated. How is it possible that their little girl would never walk again? They could not comprehend such a notion; moreover, they could not accept the prognosis. The next day, my dad went into the doctor's office looked him in the eyes, and said, "my daughter will walk again, I am not giving up on her." The doctor thought he was crazy and full of grief; however, what the doctor failed to recognize was my parents' fighting spirit.

After six months in the hospital, my parents brought me home. Both of my legs were 80 percent burned, the ligaments and muscle nonfunctional. Trying to teach me to walk again was inconceivable. I was in constant pain, yet my dad refused to give up. In fact, he thought of a brilliant plan; he decided to teach me how to walk through dancing. He thought that, for a five-year-old, it would make it fun and, somehow, dull the pain. He was right! Dad would put my little feet on his, and we would dance around the house to my favorite songs. We practiced for hours each day; and, guess what, the power of believing, against all odds, worked. In six months, I managed to start walking again.

Of course, Dad did what any dad would do - he visited the doctor who told him his daughter would never walk again; I remember as if it were yesterday. He opened the doctor's office door and let me walk in first. When the doctor saw me he froze; he was shocked. Dad looked him in the eye and said, "I told you my daughter would walk again!" Then, he took me by the hand and we left.

That moment, right there, decided my future. Can you imagine if my parents listened to the doctor? I would have never walked again and my life would be completely different now. They didn't accept the sentence prescribed by the doctors, instead choosing to fight and change my destiny. They didn't give in to the challenges but fought them with courage and faith. That's the spirit I hope to pass along to my kids and future generations. The Potinga fighting spirit!

Lesson Learned: The collapse of the Soviet Union brought about great opportunity, for free men and criminals alike.

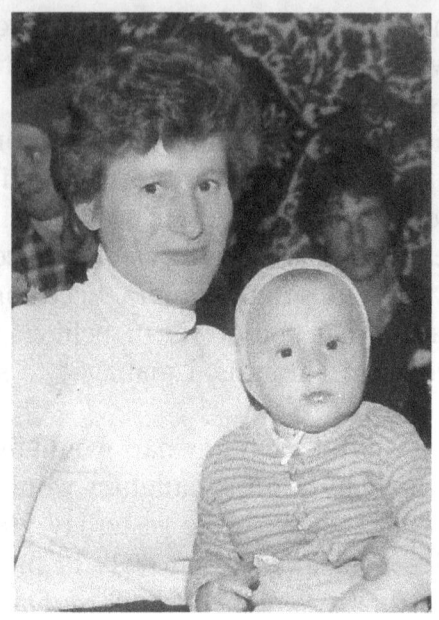

The Post-Traumatic Growth Syndrome

How do you handle obstacles? Do they serve as roadblocks or springboards? Does adversity turn your focus from getting better to getting bitter? Do you see setbacks as gifts and growth expeditors that provide the opportunity to believe in yourself, revitalize your commitment to what you want to achieve, and reassess what you are willing to sacrifice to make it happen? Adversity is one of the most powerful vigor's in life. It can make or break you; but in the end, it is up to you.

The philosopher, Frederich Nietzsche, was onto something when he said, "that which does not kill us, makes us stronger." Enduring hardship and adversity can be good for your personal growth. It can help you form a newfound appreciation for life. It will help you become more resilient and teach you to appreciate all that you have. There is an important lesson there: the harder you fight for things in life, the more value and appreciation you will attach to them. This is not exclusive to material possessions. People who have faced hardship in their life appreciate the smaller things life has to offer, such as a warm meal, a pair of shoes, petting a cat, or the laughter of a child.

I am sure many of you heard about "post-traumatic stress disorder." Conversely, there is also a condition known as "post-traumatic growth." Richard Tedeschi and Lawrence Calhoun coined the term "post-traumatic growth" to capture this phenomenon, defining it as the positive psychological change experienced because of the struggle someone experiences as a result of enduring highly challenging life circumstances. In short, it is the result of positive change in someone's life after going through a significantly stressful event. In recent years, psychologists have begun to understand the psychological processes which turn adversity into advantage. This occurs through a restructuring of mindset so that growth may occur. It is precisely when the foundational structure of the self is shaken that we are in the best position to pursue new opportunities. As Austrian psychiatrist, Viktor Frankl, put it, "when we are no longer able to change a situation, we are challenged to change ourselves."

I did not know about the notion of post-traumatic growth until I started thinking about my parents' situation; more specifically, in relation to my dad's upbringing. I have always wondered how poverty and adversity affects people, but especially how it affected my dad. Did his poor upbringing serve as motivation to work hard and aspire for a better life for his family? Was poverty and shame the root of his drive? As previously mentioned, my grandparents had twelve kids and my dad was the youngest. From the time he was born to the time he went into the army, he had a well-defined understanding of impoverishment, destitution, and shame. He lived in poverty for quite some time and grew up with the shame of being in a "poor family." No one gave him the time of the day. No one believed he and his siblings could be more than what everyone saw as the "poor Potinga family." Yet, despite the adversity, he and all his siblings did well for themselves. They all got married, had children and grandchildren, and built beautiful homes. If you ask any of my aunts, they will say they worked hard to make a different life for their kids because they did not want poverty to define them. The thing that made my dad, aunts and uncles, and grandparents different was the society they lived in. My grandparents were born during WWI, lived during WWII, communism, and socialism. These were times when there were no pathways towards a better life. They did not have the abundance of opportunities that most people take for granted today. I think of them almost as if they did not really live; they merely survived. My dad and his siblings, however, were given opportunities to make choices after Communism failed. The Iron Curtain fell and, subsequently, new doors opened wide. They experienced positive change after their many years of struggle; they experienced post-traumatic growth.

There is a story my aunts once told me during a family reunion. Four of my grandparent's girls were able to attend school. Two of the sisters would attend in the morning and the other two would attend in the afternoon. After the morning shift, the first two sisters would meet in the cemetery, which was between my grandparents' house and the school building, and swap their school uniforms and shoes with the other two so they could attend; not attending school was not an option. Even though my grandparents never finished ninth grade, they understood the importance of education. Therefore, it was imperative to them that all their children get an education and complete high school.

Lesson Learned: Use the adversity in your life as motivation, not an obstacle.

The Land of Everyone and No One

This little redhead girl was born and raised in an ex-Soviet Union country called Moldova (aka Bessarabia). Many people do not know where Moldova is, not even my husband did until he met me. When I was born, Moldova was still a communist country. My birth certificate reads "born in CCCP," or in the Union of Soviet Socialist Republics, of which Moldova was a part of. For those of you who know a bit of Soviet history from school, you'll understand that this was not the greatest place on earth; far from it. To give you a little history about Moldova, let me start from the beginning.

The origins of Moldova date back to ancient times, circa 2000 BC. A group of people known as the Dacians settled in the area where the Danube River empties into the Black Sea. This small piece of land, lying on one of the principal land routes into Europe, was invaded by successive waves of barbarians and nations. In fact, the area has had many masters over the millennia. Moldova has a long history of border disputes, struggles for freedom, and occupation by great empires – from the Roman Empire (as part of Dacia), to the Ottoman Empire, to most recently, Russia.

This region was an integral part of the Romanian principality of Moldavia until 1812, when it was ceded to Russia by its suzerain, the sultan of the Ottoman Empire. Bessarabia remained a province of the Russian Empire until after World War I, when it became part of Greater Romania. It then reverted to Russian control in 1940–41 and again after World War II, when it was joined to a strip of former Ukrainian territory, the Moldavian Autonomous Soviet Socialist Republic, on the left bank of the Dniester River to form the Moldavian Soviet Socialist Republic. Upon the collapse of the Soviet Union in August 1991, the republic declared its independence on August 27th, 1991 and took the name Moldova. Despite Moldova's independence, the Soviet culture and Russian influence lingered for another 20 years; I believe it still does to this day, to some extent. Moldova's geographic location is both a blessing and a curse. Depending on the state of affairs between the West and the East, Moldova either serves as a buffer on the frontlines or as a bridge to partnership.

There are multiple factors that divide Moldova, but the main one today is ethnic division. It started with the program of resettlement, carried out by Joseph Stalin and his Communists. Stalin carried out the program by relocating Moldovans to other parts of the Soviet Union and ethnic Russians and Ukrainians to Moldova. After

Stalin's death in 1953, Nikita Khushchev ended the Stalinist resettlement program. However, the Russification program of immigration continued, with Russian remaining the official language of Moldova and the Cyrillic alphabet until 1991. Moldovans were prohibited from using the colors of the Romanian flag as part of their flag until the collapse of Soviet Union.

Moldova is a cocktail of Eastern European ethnicities: Moldovan 75.1%, Romanian 7%, Ukrainian 6.6%, Gagauz 4.6%, Russian 4.1%, Bulgarian 1.9%, other 0.8% (Census, 2014). As long as I can remember, the subject of ethnicity has been the topic of debate between the Moldovan people. Are we Romanians, Moldovans, or Russians? Do we want to be part of the European Union (EU) or remain under Russian influence? These questions have been lingering for more than thirty years and remain unanswered today. On one hand, the older generations want to be part of Russia due to the nostalgic sentiment around the Soviet Union. On the other hand, the younger generation wants to be part of the EU due to the opportunities and prosperity that the union brings. This concept of, "one leg in Romania and one leg in Russia," only suppresses Moldova's political, economic, and social development. Moldova will never be united towards a common goal if people do not come together as one nation.

Another issue causing division in the country is language. Moldova was reunified with Romania in 1918 and then annexed by the Soviet Union in 1940. The linguistic issue has its roots from Soviet times when the Soviets created an artificial alphabet, different from the obsolete Romanian Cyrillic. Moldova has been subject to a tug-of-war between

Romania and Russia, compounded by Russia's designs on its breakaway region of Transnistria, into which Moscow funnels cash in payouts and subsidies, and stations hundreds of soldiers. During my childhood, I was confused about the never-ending language debate. Some would say we should speak Russian, while others would argue that we should speak Romanian. There was even a third opinion: as a sovereign country, people should speak Moldovan. However, this language does not technically exist, as it was made up by a soviet regime. When going to the store or the bazaar, you would never know whether the seller spoke Russian or Romanian. Once, while in a shop, I asked the clerk in Romanian the cost of a kilogram of tomatoes. She gave me a hard look and responded in Russian with an attitude. I knew she could speak Romanian, she just refused to do so.

While Moldova continues to struggle with its identity crisis, its rich culture is something all its citizens can stand by. Moldova's culture goes back to Roman times, with the ancient overlay, colored by Byzantine, Magyar, Serbian, Ottoman, Russian, and Soviet influences. Ever since the 19th century, European and French elements have been added, forming a varied, lively, and resilient lifestyle expressed in traditions, festivals, the arts, music, dance, and literature. Elements of folk culture, such as wood carving and embroidery, are shared with other Balkan countries. However, many aspects, such as pottery decoration and the 2,000-year-old Doina lyrical songs, are unique to Moldova.

Lesson Learned: The unification of people, under freedom, makes a country prosperous.

The Land of Wine

I loved autumn in Moldova for many reasons. It brought with it cool weather and the harvest; I would often help my mother pick out the fruits and vegetables from our garden. Even more so, I loved that this was the season during which wine was made. Autumn in Moldova means villages are filled with the fresh aroma of fermenting wine. My parents would wake up at dawn and go to the vineyard to pick the fruit; sometimes, I would go along to help. Dad inspected the grapes and if there was a good crop he would say, "we have a beautiful autumn this year. It's warm and good, and the grapes are ripe and only good for making a good wine." I used to run through the rows of grape vines with my hair down and sun in my face and choose the grapes I wanted to eat; it was the best time. After the harvest, we would return home and prepare for the difficult but rewarding work.

The crates of grapes are processed by pressing and crushing the grapes in two barrels and left to ferment. The entire process is a real art and my dad did everything with his hands. "Every grape is important," he would say. "You must feel its personality as you squeeze it and turn it into juice and pulp in your hands." Fermentation lasts anywhere from five to eight days. During this process and before the wine matures, the grapes transform into grape must, which is sweet grape juice.

The sweet fragrance of the grapes permeated the air around every village in Moldova. Due to the short timeframe in which the fermentation process occurs, the aroma can only be enjoyed for a few weeks each year. The wine making process was the favorite moment for kids due to the grape juice. All my cousins would visit us in Moldova just to get a taste of the grape must; it's actually the most organic grape juice you can have. Even though the wine fermentation is not complete, and the wine still isn't matured, the must has some alcohol in it (circa 1%). I remember one year, after dad had finished crushing the grapes and had placed them in barrels for fermentation, my cousins, my brother, and I decided to try the new must. We crept during the night so my parents would not catch us. We had a little too much, however, because when Dad found us next to the barrel, we were giggling uncontrollably. It was just 1% alcohol, but it was enough for a bunch of scallywags like us to get tipsy. Needless to say, we were grounded and never attempted to drink grape must without Dad's permission again. But it certainly makes for a good story, which we recount repeatedly at family reunions.

Every household in Moldova has a cellar to store wine. This is, by far, my husband's favorite feature. My uncle's cellar has matured several varieties of wine; pour pink wine out of the barrel, it is his Rosé or Cabernet; pour white, and it's Pinot Gris or Sauvignon Blanc; pour red, it's Pinot Noir or Merlot. Moldovan wines have better characteristics than those more famously known around the world, such as Italian or French derivatives. Moldova has great geographic micro-areas and a favorable climate. Additionally, the country has several pieces of land that contain chernozem, which is fertile, black soil containing a plethora of fantastic mineral elements. With the help of these environmental conditions, Moldova grows some of the highest quality grapes in the world.

Wine is deeply rooted in Moldovan culture, and its history begins in 3000 BC with the first vines recorded being around 7000 BC. They were appreciated in ancient times by the Romans, and a major source of export revenue for Moldova during the Middle Ages. It was even, occasionally, used as a trophy after fights. Moldova has 112,000 hectares of vineyard planted with over 50 types of technical varieties. There are 142 wineries, which include about a dozen that offer tours and tastings. It is a national product of Moldova; the underground cellars are legendary and recognized as the largest in the world by the Guinness Book of World Records.

These vineyards are characterized in many ways. They are known, in part, to be mysterious given the expansiveness of the underground routes. They have also been described as "glorious" by well-known personalities who have visited them. But, most importantly, they are authentic due to their presence in the household of every Moldovan. Milestii-Mici is the largest underground wine cellar in the world. The collection consists of over 2 million bottles stretching underground for 250 km (of which, only 120 km are currently in use). The second largest winery in the world, Cricova, is also located in Moldova. It boasts a mere 120 km of labyrinthine roadways. These tunnels have existed under Cricova since the 15th century, when limestone was quarried to help build Chisinau, the capital of Moldova. They were later converted into the underground wine emporium they are today in the 1950s.

Lesson Learned: Nowhere in the world you will find wine like in Moldova.

No Materialism, Just Love

I was two years old when I entered kindergarten. Back in Soviet times, maternity leave was two years. The government determined that the absence of a mother in the home for the first two years was detrimental for a child's development. People often ask me if there was anything good about growing up under the rule of a communist government. Admittedly, there were a few good things, maternity leave being one of them. Moldova has retained the policy today, and I believe it speaks to the strong support the country's leadership has towards new mothers, especially considering it is one of the poorest countries in eastern Europe.

Since my mother had to stay home to take care of me for those first two years, my dad was the only person in the family that was working. He worked for the city as a driver on a waste collection truck. He was, and still is, the hardest working man I have ever met in my life and who I took my work ethic from. He would often tell me, "nothing in this world is free, not even the air we breathe. If someone is offering you something free, that means you are the product, and they will make the profit one way or another." As the youngest child of a poor family, he was familiar with the concept of hunger and poverty. However, he strived to give my brother and I the best life he could. I think he succeeded!

As I remember, my childhood was filled with smiles and laughs. This was not the result of materialistic possessions, but the love my parents, grandparents, and extended family provided. Nowadays, I believe the script has flipped and parents attempt to compensate for an absence of love and attention with materialistic things. That is a big problem in our modern society. My parents were poor before and after they got married. They both married young; my dad was seventeen and my mom, nineteen. They did not have a house to live in. They did not have reliable full-time jobs. They did not have their parents to help them. They only had themselves and the love they had for one another. That was enough to keep them together for forty years, and they are still going strong to this day.

There are memories that I will never forget; memories that, many times, remind me to be grateful for what I have now that I did not have then. One of these memories is when I was four years old during a Christmas event held by my kindergarten school. I was assigned a song to sing and the teacher asked our parents to dress us in white - white shoes, white stockings, white dress, and a white hair bow. My poor mom came home crying to my dad; she felt hopeless because we didn't have the money to buy all of the necessary pieces of the outfit. Fortunately, my mom is wise, talented, and always knows how to get the job done. She remembered that she had a white bed sheet she could use to make my dress and bow. She called my aunt, Stepanida, and asked her if I could borrow my cousin's white shoes. My mom handmade me a white outfit and decorated my shoes with handmade paper and glitter Christmas decorations. It was beautiful! I still look at pictures from that event and think to myself, "Mom knows how to make everything better, even in poor situations." When I was 7 years old, both of my parents started to work for collective farms. These farms were launched in 1927 by Joseph Stalin with the goal of rapid industrialization and collectivization of agriculture.

The aim was to erase all traces of the capitalist movement that had entered under "the New Economic Policy," and to transform the Soviet Union as quickly as possible, without regard to cost, into an industrialized and socialist state. To do this, Stalin ordered the confiscation of individuals' land, tools, and animals. The kolkhoz (collective farm) thus replaced the family farm. The state would decide the types of crops to be produced, as well as the quantity, the salaries paid to the individuals for their work, the price the crops would be sold for, and how much of the profits would go to the state. Farmers who resisted this mandate were persecuted, exiled, and killed. Consequently, a food shortage came about, and the rations were barely enough to feed a family. My brother and I were lucky, because we only had to experience the hardships of the collective farm system for ten years. My grandparents, consequently, experienced it throughout their entire lives and my parents, for thirty years. From those ten years of my life, I have very vivid memories of never having enough food or clothes.

Another story that stayed with me for years was the early morning "bread line." I was four years old and my brother was eight. Every morning, we got up at 5:30am to be in line at the store by 5:45am for bread. The cart with bread would arrive at 6:15am, so we had to make sure we were in the line on time, otherwise, we would be left with no bread for that day. The bread was freshly baked with a delicious smell that would make you hungry instantly. We had to present coupons to get the bread; these coupons, which were pieces of multi-colored paper, were given to us on a monthly basis so we could purchase various items. The number of coupons distributed per month to each family was dependent on the number of family members they had. I knew we were supposed to get two loaves of bread because we were a family of four - half a loaf of bread per member. Everything was accounted for and distributed equally. If you missed the car of bread in the morning, there would be no more until the next day. Sometimes, during bad weather or because of government error, families had to wait several days. This put a significant burden on families because bread was used as part of the appetizer, main course and, occasionally, even dessert. To make matters worse, stores shelves were constantly depleted of anything remotely sustaining.

What saved us from perpetual hunger was our garden. After Stalin's reign, every household had a garden with veggies and fruit that we used to feed ourselves throughout the year. During the summer months, we thrived on fresh tomatoes, cucumbers, zucchini, carrots, and onions. During the fall months, we survived on potatoes and beans. During the harsher winter months, we resorted to eating food from jars. Mom conserved fruit and vegetables during the summer and fall so we would have food to eat during the dreary winters; she also saved chickens and ducks. Everything was homemade from scratch and healthy; but, having healthy food was not of primary concern. The main concern was food supply. As previously mentioned, you could not just walk into a supermarket anytime of the day and get whatever you wanted. The supplies were exhausted or limited, in which case there was a line to purchase it. It could take up to several days to replace the supply of food. Comparably, it could take a few years to purchase bigger ticket items like furniture or cars.

Lesson Learned: Love and some food is all that a child needs to have a happy childhood.

Early School Years

Many of my foreign friends often ask me about my childhood. They particularly want to know what the Soviet school system was like: what subjects we studied, what uniform we wore, how we spent our time after school, and how we spent our three months of summer vacations.

When compared to the school system in the United States, Moldova had a very different approach to education. In fact, the schools in Russia, Ukraine, Armenia, Kazakhstan, and many other Soviet republics were one in the same. They all had a large blackboard in the front accompanied by chalk and a wet cloth. The teacher's desk sat in front of the blackboard and faced the rest of the classroom. Above the blackboard hung a big portrait of Lenin and in some classrooms, there was also a large, round clock.

There were three rows of wooden desks with benches or chairs; each desk sat two kids which were assigned by the teacher. Some teachers would sit the troublesome kids in front, while the rest of the class would be seated in the back. In the elementary grades, teachers usually sat shorter kids closer to the front and taller kids towards the back. During the Soviet regime, we started attending school at the age of seven. From seven to ten we repeated the same subjects, but they became more complicated each year as we progressed to a new grade level. What made it a little easier was that they were taught by the same teacher. At the age of ten, we had to say goodbye to our first teacher and move to another level, where we learned different subjects each taught by a different teacher.

There were many different subjects we learned in school that have never been heard of in the U.S. and other countries. One of those subjects was called "the labor." It was a subject where, for the majority of the daily lessons, boys and girls were taught separately. Girls were taught to cook and sew. Boys learned woodworking and metalworking skills. Labor classrooms were equipped with a workshop for the boys and the necessary equipment. For the girls, the school had a wonderful room full of tools and ingredients used for baking and materials for sowing. This subject was so useful because it taught us the essential skills of everyday life. I genuinely loved it when I sewed my first skirt and apron.

America - The Architect of My Destiny

The first two years of school I had to wear a uniform consisting of a dress and an apron. The apron was regularly black, but occasionally white for holidays and special occasions. The dress was white, often lacy or trimmed, with a removable lace collar and cuff covers (they were sewn on with a running stitch); these were typically removed, laundered, and sewn back on once or, for flusher weeks, twice a week. I had one uniform set that lasted me a year, or sometimes two, depending on how quickly I grew. All the girls in school looked identical, except that each had her own personalized bow in her hair and on her collar, as well as laces on her apron. Regardless, every part of our uniform was expected to be nice, clean, and suitable.

Because of the general deficit of everything in Moldova, there wasn't much variety available in school supplies. Each child had access to the same handful of products. My books, pencils, rules, and notebooks looked the same as everyone else's. As kids, we used to get shoes once a year at the start of the school year, and that's assuming we were lucky and not growing too fast. For the start of second grade, my mother bought me a pair of beautiful, dark red shoes; they were shiny with a little flower design on them. I was the happiest child in the world. I used to walk with them every day to school. If I got dust or dirt on them, I wiped them clean right away. I wanted them to last as long as possible. This was not only because they were beautiful, but because I knew my parents could not afford to get me another pair until I grew out of them, or they completely fell apart.

Like I said, there were a few good things within communism. Besides two years maternity leave, with pay and job retention (returning to work was a communist guarantee), another positive was the education system. Of course, Stalin had swiftly eradicated the well-educated and abruptly executed those useful idiots he thought to be a threat, in order to prevent an uprising that could or would challenge the Bolshevik one. Therefore, Soviet schools, like the one I attended, had their fair share of problems and teething pains while trying to fill the void left in the wake of genocide. The curriculum was infused with the "appropriate" ideology: teachers presented history through the Marxist-Leninist prism, covering the struggle of social classes as being defined by material condition. What worked well, however, amongst all that misery was high expectations, written and oral exams, memorization, and, above all, the literary principal and math. The USSR adopted the 19th-century German educational model and then mixed in its own content. Such education systems worked, arguably even producing the very people who eventually ended up challenging the Soviet state (see Aleksandr Solzhenitsyn's *Gulag Archipelago*).

Lesson Learned: The appreciation of a quality school system.

The Iron Curtain

Being limited in what you could afford was the norm in Moldova. Even though people strived to improve their lives, it was close to impossible. As a little girl, I remember my parents being frugal; you just did not throw things away. Old coats could always be remodeled, and nails could be reused. Glass jars from pickles would hold next years' jam. To give you a further illustration, let's look at the life cycle of pantyhose (tights). To get a pair of pantyhose, you had to know someone at the store or bargain in exchange for something else. You wear them, but sooner or later you get a hole in them. What do you do if you are living in the USSR? First thing is reach for the nail polish. You seal the run with clear nail polish. Then when you come home, you fix the hole. There were even special hooks which were used for mending tights. You use that pair of tights until you can no longer hide the holes. What do you do afterwards? Toss them? Absolutely not. You wear them in the winter under trousers! Nobody can see you have tights with holes if you wear trousers on top of them, right? And an extra layer does keep you warm.

We were not allowed access to imported consumer goods, especially those manufactured in the United States. East of what was known as the "Iron Curtain," the Soviet economic system called for self-sufficiency in all matters. This included everything from making our own bread to clothes to furniture to cars. Meanwhile, the countries surrounding the Soviet Union had become economic powerhouses, producing consumer goods that vastly improved the quality of life for citizens who could afford them. With German cars, French perfume, Italian wines and British-made appliances, Western Europeans were living the good life compared to their Soviet counterparts. The Soviet countries had gotten used to long queues and shortages of everything.

I personally did not have a lot of clothes or shoes growing up, and whatever I did own was precious to me. The pair of shoes I did have were impeccably cleaned every day. My clothes were washed by hand, ironed, and placed on hangers for good keeping. I washed my socks and undergarments every night after a bath to make sure we had clean clothes for the next day of school. We never threw away socks with holes - we mended them. Things like Coca-Cola, Levi's, Marlboro, Nikes and Turbo gums were some of the contraband goods from abroad that were in great demand. The problem was that these goods were scarce. It was not easy to get your hands on the famous beverage, Coca-Cola, as it was not sold in shops. Often it came down to how "connected" a buyer was. Soviet war-hero and General, Zhukov, used his unique position to ask General Dwight D. Eisenhower to supply him a special brew of Coca-Cola. Not to impede his ideological allegiances by being seen drinking the capitalist beverage, General Zhukov demanded his supply of Coca-Cola come in unmarked bottles decorated with a red star, the symbol of the Red Army, on the crown cap. These were the lengths people would go to in order to have a taste of this drink. I would bet most people from the Soviet Union remember when and where they had their first soda; my first was Mountain Dew in a can. I was eight years old when I begged my dad to buy me one. It was pricey for those times. When he purchased me a can, I thought I was the coolest kid in the neighborhood. Other kids were begging me to share just a sip of this magnificent drink. The deficit, the desire to try and have unavailable things made us appreciate the little we had very dearly. Waist was not a word in our vocabulary.

Lesson Learned: You will never have everything in life; but, when you have what you want, don't forget to cherish and appreciate it.

Chapter 2

THE ROOTS

"Never forget where you came from, but never let that hold you back from where you want to go."
- Unknown

America Through A Soviet Lens

Growing up, America was a dream. A faraway land that I only knew about via TV shows and magazines. It was a vague, limited view because Moldova was barely recovering after the collapse of the Soviet Union. We were not allowed to learn what real American culture was during Soviet times. America through a Soviet Union lens was seen as wicked, too open-minded, and even toxic for Soviet citizens. But at the same time, Soviet people were a little envious, and most held private admiration for the productivity, organizational efficiency, and technological sophistication of American industry, agriculture, and culture.

Isolated from the rest of the world, many Soviet people wanted to know what life was like on the other side of the Iron Curtain. Their curiosity peaked, they tested every one of their assumptions, shaped by Soviet propaganda, about the United States. More than anything, they wanted to satisfy the basic human urge to know another person, swap life stories with a stranger, learn about others' experiences, and make new friends.

Soviet attitudes toward the American socio-economic system were an odd mixture of envy and contempt. Everyone wanted to live the "American dream", but they could not say it out loud, it was forbidden. When the Soviet Union collapsed in 1991, Soviet citizens were free to travel and learn about the world. Communist propaganda and its ideology were no longer a concern, and people, for the first time, were able to form an independent opinion. Their eyes were wide open. They could travel abroad without any "special permission" from the government. The freedom they gained was often too much to handle; they wanted to do so much, but they knew so little.

It was a new world with new possibilities. On one hand, the communist claws had been removed, and on the other hand, the vast, chaotic unknown was left in its place. Everything that constituted the existence of the united republics disappeared virtually overnight: the central committee of the communist party, the Soviet state system of socialism, Marxist ideology, and central planning. Moldova confronted many of the challenges head on: economic decline, political turmoil, and inter-ethnic discord. People were asking, East or West? Which course to choose? Do we stay close to Russia, or do we venture into Europe? The questions were answered very quickly.

Once communism had failed and the Soviet Union ceased to exist, we could venture out into the world, and the world could venture into us. We could get access to international media, movies, music, books, and magazines. The fear of getting arrested if you are caught with a dollar in your pocket or an American newspaper was over. So, Hollywood invaded Moldova. The first American show I watched was the movie "Dallas," with everyone's favorite character, J.R. Ewing (Larry Hagman). J.R. was a sort of Texas cowboy and an oil tycoon. In my visions he was a controversial character caught between a shrewd, ruthless, conniving Texas oil baron/tycoon and a sympathetic, generous man. His love for his family and the lengths he would go for them was admirable. His famous phrase that stuck with me was: "Anything worth having is worth going for - all the way." I think this was the moment I fell in love with Texas. I loved the ranch houses, the horses, the cowboy hats and boots, the simple, humble life; all of it was magnificent. I remember my dad always wanted a cowboy hat and pair of boots, and indeed he got them when he visited Texas for the first time. I know it sounds cliché, but we were so hungry for American television, it was like candy. The second show that introduced me to American culture was "Friends." I believe it was 1998 when I saw the first episode and I was instantly hooked I was in love with the idea of a group of friends, young and carefree, meeting on a regular basis in a Manhattan coffee shop to chit chat and drink coffee - I mean what else can be better?! All the characters were unique and layered. Depending on the situation, you'd find yourself relating with different characters at different points in the show, and in the end, you end up connecting with the entire cast. I remember at one point I asked my mom to allow me to get "The Rachel" haircut, which was Jennifer Aniston's famous style. Friends represented a simpler time — before smartphones, social media, and apps dominated our attention, time, and friendships. The show gave me an idea of what America could be for a young, aspiring person. A country where a person can be free, and I mean really free. Free to be who they want, and to achieve what they want. To be one's authentic self without any prejudice. I was in love with America. I knew it was where my future lay.

Lesson Learned: It's okay to think outside the box and outside your borders.

There's No Clean Breakup

Moldovan citizens realized that, even though the Soviet Union had collapsed, Russian authorities still wanted to maintain their grip on former republics, including Moldova. Moldovan people wanted to be completely free from Russian influence, but it was difficult to achieve.

The broken economic ties between Soviet entities had serious repercussions on people's living conditions. This in turn made the political situation in Moldova unstable, and forced Moldova to plead for economic cooperation from Russia. Besides Russia's economic power over Moldova, there was another reason for Russia to want to keep Moldova under its authority; Transnistria.

Transnistria is a territory in Moldova that is not recognized by any sovereign state. This territory declared independence from Moldova in 1990 and fought a war to maintain it two years later. Transnistria has a constitution, a flag, and even a coat of arms. Portraits of Putin and Lenin can be bought and sold on the city streets of Tiraspol, the de facto capital. Storefronts and street signs almost exclusively feature the Cyrillic script (both for Russian and Romanian), and even the flag still bears the infamous hammer-and-sickle. However, you won't find this region on many maps, and not a single member of the United Nations recognizes its existence.

When Moldova broke away from the Soviet Union in 1990, Transnistria became home to many Russians and Russian speakers who felt political and cultural isolation in the new republic. They declared independence, hoping to establish a socialist republic and remain part of the Soviet Union. A war ensued against Moldova, which ended in a ceasefire nearly two years later. The Soviet Union had already crumbled by then, and the conflict never fully resolved even though Moldova granted Transnistria a measure of autonomy. The Transnistrian people are stuck in a country that doesn't exist. One notable element of Russian involvement in the conflict in Moldova was the stationing of the then Soviet (now Russian) 14th army on the northern bank of the Dniester River. The stationing of Russian troops in Transnistria granted Russia "hard power" in Moldova. Russia additionally wants to maintain influence in Moldova via Transnistria due to its fear of the eastward expansion of western institutions such as NATO and the European Union. Like Abkhazia is to Georgia, and South Ossetia is to Ukraine, such is the geopolitical importance of Transnistria, to both Russia and NATO.

Lesson Learned: Once big nations fall, little countries have a hard time finding their footing again.

Vodka in the Attic

As a child, I loved summertime. We either spent it in the village where Grandma lives or in Russia where my aunt and cousin live. In either case, it was a wonderful time replete with great memories. My grandma lives in Radeni, about 70km from our home near Chisinau, so we used to visit often and spend a lot of summers there. My Grandma from my mothers side is an epic human being. Not only does she love us dearly, but she is one of the strongest people I know in my life. She had a difficult childhood and equally hard adulthood, but she managed to keep the goodness alight in her all these years. You never sense an ounce of bitterness in her, ever. It has always amazed me how a person can go through so much and still be kind and loving. She and her six siblings were orphaned when both of her parents passed away a couple of months apart. They died of starvation and sickness, during war and famine, when she was only seven years old. At one point, she was left alone in the house because all her other siblings had to go looking for food. Her older brother even went so far to beg for food on trains going to Ukraine. He did this until a woman found him sleeping on the streets and adopted him. He reunited with Grandma and their remaining siblings 50 years later, which was a very touching moment for our family.

Grandma married at the age of sixteen to my grandpa who was a very bitter man and didn't treat her nicely; but she never left him, no matter the hardship. After he passed away 10 years ago, she was left alone in the village. She has a big household with agricultural land, vineyards, animals, and a lovely home garden where she grows her fruit and veggies. She is 85 years old and she still climbs the ladder to the attic where she stores food, and still makes homemade vodka which we call samagon. She is just a rock star. Every time I ask her, "Grandma, how are you doing?" she always replies, "still on my feet, thanks to God!" She never, ever complains about her age, pain, life; not once have I heard her say something hurts. I have the best memories of time spent with her in the village. It was a simple and humbling experience but so rewarding. We ran after the chickens and ducks, or went with her to the land and ran through the rows of grape vines. If we got sick, she had the best homemade remedies. Let's say we caught a fever; she would give us a good massage with vinegar, bundle us up in a blanket, dip our socks in vinegar, and by morning, the fever would go away. If it was a cough, she would get a big white turnip, make a hole in the middle, and put honey in it. In a couple of hours, the turnip and honey make a natural cough syrup, which we would drink until the cough went away. She has a remedy for everything and I still use them to this day - even my Australian husband loves these! He is amazed by the positive, potent effects of these homemade remedies.

   A great memory I have of my grandma is her home made vodka. One year I was visiting from the U.S. and, knowing she makes homemade vodka every year, I asked her to give me a liter to take home with me. My American friends go bananas for this alcohol and they always ask me to bring some back. So, she climbed up to the attic and brought down a five-liter bottle of vodka. I looked at her and said in Romanian, "Grandma! I can't take so much, it doesn't fit." She smiled and replied. "Honey, put it under the bus seat." I started laughing. "Grandma, I don't go to America by bus, but by plane!" She looked at me disappointedly. "That's a shame, what are you going to do with just one liter of vodka?" It was a priceless moment, one we still laugh about to this day; but that's my grandma - funny, goofy, and loving all at the same time. After I returned to the U.S., my mom called me in a panic. She said, "honey, did you drink or give Grandma's vodka to any of your friends?" I responded. "No, not yet," and she said, "honey, Grandma called and was worried about the batch of vodka she gave you - she doesn't remember which batch the liter came from. Please pour a bit in a glass and light it on fire; if it doesn't ignite, you are okay, but if it does, add some water or juice, the vodka is too strong." Luckily, it didn't ignite, so I didn't have to add water; but this is the kind of vodka my 85-year-old grandma makes.

Lesson Learned: Be careful! If the homemade vodka ignites, add some water to it.

The Duck and Vacuum

Summers spent in Russia were different but fun. My aunt has lived there for the last 50 years, and every other summer my parents would put us on a train, alongside my cousins, and send us to her. It was a soviet train and took approximately two days to get to Moscow. The party consisted of me, my brother, Alex, my cousin, Yuri, my other cousin, Inga, and her brother, Igor. It was a blast, the five of us in one train cabin, playing games and telling stories for two days straight. Once we arrived in Moscow, my uncle, who was a Russian police officer, would pick us up and drive us to Ryazan (100km from Moscow) where they lived. There we would join three more cousins, Oxana, Natalia, and Sasha. I was the youngest cousin, so they had to take care of me whenever we were playing in the neighborhood. Many times they'd get frustrated but they didn't have much of a choice, as my aunty made them responsible. My favorite cousin was Sasha. He was this big, tall Russian kid with the kindest and gentlest heart. He always defended me and never left me behind.

To be able to go on this trip, however, my brother and I had to be on good behavior and have good grades in school all year long. One year, my parents bought a bunch of ducklings we had to take care of. A few days before the trip, my mom said to me, "I am going to the store to get some things for your trip, you take care of the ducks. Make sure they are all in one piece when I get home if you want to go to Russia." They were held in a big container while they were still small, and it had a big, wire fence so the vultures could not get them. Noon meant it was time to feed. I believe I was eight years old at the time, a little skinny girl with, as I'm sure you can imagine, not much strength to lift a wire fence. While I was lifting it up to feed the ducklings, I accidentally dropped it on top of one, killing it and injuring the leg of another I burst into tears; one, because I killed one of my favorite ducks, and two because my chances of going to Russia were all of a sudden looking slim. What do I do now? How do I hide the evidence of the accidental crime? Well, a "secret mission" was formed in my mind. First, I needed to bury the deceased duck. Second, I needed to attend to, and then hide, the injured duck. I buried the one duckling and proceeded to attend to the other; I took a piece of material and wrapped it's injured foot. Okay, now where do I hide it? I realized under the table, where Mom stored the ironing equipment for our clothes, was a box with the vacuum inside. Well, this eight-year-old girl thought, "that's a perfect place to hide the evidence"... so I did. I hid the duck in the vacuum. When Mom came home, she didn't even bother counting the ducks, and instead started preparing my brother and I for the trip. While she was ironing our clothes, she heard a duck sound. She looked at me quizzically and said, "where is that sound coming from?" I felt guilty but didn't show it on my face and said, "Mom it's coming from outside." I left for Russia with my brother and cousins as planned, but a few days later my aunty got a call from my mom. She asked to speak to me about something, even though I knew she discovered the duck in the vacuum. I picked up the phone and she said "so... Miss Doctor, we found the duck in the vacuum - good job attending to the wounded foot - but the duck nearly died of hunger." I exhaled deeply;

thank God the duck was still alive! My mom laughed and told me never to lie or do such a thing again. This was the length an eight year old me was willing to go just to spend the summer with her cousins. It's a heck of a story, which I am reminded of often, especially at family reunions.

Lesson Learned: If you think you can hear a duck quacking, you probably can.

The Vision

Envision sitting down writing a script for your life, only to step into a movie where it's your reality. Is it as you imagined? Are you the main character or just an extra, lost in the masses? I've always believed that life truly is what we make of it. The stories we tell ourselves can either liberate or enslave us. The script I've been writing for myself since I was a kid has always placed me as the central character of my story. I didn't want anyone to dictate my journey for me. I wanted to be able to change the narrative anytime I so choose. As the great U.S. President, Abraham Lincoln, once said, "The best way to predict your future is to create it." And so, I started to create my future very early on.

I knew since seventh grade I wanted to go to law school or study economics. I always imagined myself dressed in a business suit, holding a folder with documents and attending business meetings. I knew I would get there one day through hard work and perseverance. In eleventh grade, I had to decide what college I wanted to attend. This was a crucial moment in my life and for my family because I was the first person in my family to attend college. My dad had been dreaming of this day for years. Even though he finished high school with a red diploma (the highest achievement one could have in the Soviet Union) he was not able to finish college. He attended a year of Kharkiv University (in Ukraine) but he was not able to finish due to financial difficulties. Seeing me attend and graduate from college was his dream. As cheesy as it sounds, I loved to study, I always have since I was a kid. Mom used to say she never had to sit with me to do homework, I was independent from very early on. When the time came to choose the university I wanted to attend, my dad and I visited the best Moldova had to offer. He never pressured me towards a particular degree or field but he always said, "honey, you need to choose a degree that is going to provide you with an income for the rest of your life." He used to say, "a man can find a manual job such as a mechanic or a truck driver, for a woman it is much harder. Women need to be educated and be independent because life is unpredictable." And I am so happy for my dad's wisdom and guidance. He was, and still is, my mentor.

So after visiting five universities, I set my sights on the Academy of Economic Studies in Chisinau. It was the best school for economics and finance in Moldova and had many faculties and degrees to choose from. After some brainstorming, I chose the faculty of Economics with concentrations in Finance and Banking. I could see myself in that business suit, holding a financial report and chairing a meeting in my mind. I already created the image in my head, now I just had to live it. I passed the admission exams without any hick-ups, and soon became an economics student.

The university system in Moldova is very different from that of the United States. A full-time student in Moldova does eight to ten classes a semester (as opposed to four or five, typically, in the U.S.), and you don't get to choose your classes or time, the schedule is created for you by the faculty. Lastly, libraries are your best friend. Even though it was 2004, access to the internet and computers was... problematic. I didn't have a computer back then. If I needed information for a project, I could go freely to the library, or wait for the allotted 1.5hrs per week of internet time in the computer lab.

I actually preferred the libraries. I love the smell of books, to have a hard copy of a book in my hand; it makes me appreciate the information more. Maybe that's where my love of reading was born. My favorite hobby in college was grabbing a good cup of coffee and an equally captivating book, finding a spot in nature, and simply enjoying it. That's all I needed for happiness and a reprieve from studying! The four years were challenging and fun all at the same time. For the first three years I couldn't work; I attended school from 8 am to 5 pm, Monday through Friday, and sometimes Saturday. There was no time for work or any other activities, school was my main focus. Maybe because I knew how hard my parents worked to pay for it and my everyday expenses. I had better make the best of it! My last year was lighter, both in terms of classes and workload. I was writing my graduation thesis, so I was also able to work part time. My hard-working parents paid for all of my study and living expenses until my fourth and final year, when I was able to pay my way with the money I made in the U.S. (more about this later on in the chapter).

Not having access to the internet or a computer made me work harder. I had to spend hours in the library just to write a paper for a project; then, to type the paper, I had to wait in the computer lab queue. It was impossible to know how much all that hard work would pay off in the future. It taught me resilience, patience, and to not be afraid to spend hours looking for the information I needed. Even today, I enjoy sitting in the library reading or researching an interesting subject. I think it's very rewarding.

Lesson Learned: If you can imagine and visualize something, you can probably achieve it with hard work and determination.

Higher Education or Socialism

The number of students in Moldova has been steadily increasing since the collapse of the Soviet Union in 1991. Higher education in Moldova is popular, and academic degrees are in high demand. After the Soviet Union collapsed, the population of Moldova was left jobless. Many people in Moldova could not afford to attend university during Soviet times, and the jobs to be found, in factories or working in collective farming as my parents did, didn't require a degree. Once the Soviet Union collapsed, however, all those jobs were gone, and people quickly found themselves in despair. In some ways it was a good thing; it motivated my dad to start his own business. But for those left without a job, without the ability to start a business, or any means of income, it was a very bad thing.

For my parents' generation, the experience served as a tremendous lesson to make sure their children were well educated, with at least a bachelor's degree. The emphasis on getting a degree was so intense that almost every one of my generation and the generation after me in my family have, at minimum, a bachelor's degree. Having a degree is not only a necessary requirement in order to get a chance to find a job (which isn't guaranteed) but it's also a status symbol. It's all about who you know. If you have someone that works in the Ministry of Finance, maybe you have a better chance of getting a decent job; but a decent job doesn't necessarily equate to decent pay.

To give you an idea, the salary that university faculty receive — $120 - 200 U.S. dollars per month — is barely enough to cover the cost of food, even if one eats at the on-campus cafeteria. Can you imagine having a masters or doctoral degree and getting paid a measly $120 a month? Yes, the cost of living in Moldova is lower compared to the rest of Europe, but $120 each month is not enough to live on, even in Moldova. Faced with political instability, collapsing incomes, and swiftly rising unemployment, people began emigrating from Moldova - on a large scale - from the late 1990's through the early 2010's.

The Moldovan Intelligence and Security Service has estimated between 600,000 to 1 million Moldovan citizens (almost 25 percent of our 4.4 million population) are working abroad, some illegally. Countries such as Russia, Italy, France, Romania, Portugal, Spain, Greece, Turkey, and Israel offer the most appealing job opportunities for my fellow Moldovans. The post-Soviet wave of unemployment forced many qualified technicians and professionals to go abroad and take up illegal employment far below their qualifications. The unemployment rate in Moldova today is estimated to be around 25 percent. The widespread urge to escape from dismal economic conditions is overwhelming. According to a survey of the younger Moldovans by the Center of Sociological, Political Science, and Psychological

Investigation and Analysis (CIVIS), 52 percent of teenagers want to go abroad to get a job. Responding to a separate question, 15 percent of the teenagers surveyed would like to emigrate permanently.

Until November 2020, Moldova was the only European country with a ruling party that still considered itself communist, and where new Lenin statues were still being erected (in Transnistria). The communist politicians do not seem to view the emigration of young Moldovans (who do not vote for them anyway) as problematic. In the words of one official, "emigration is better than revolution." As Aleksandr Solzhenitsyn said, "socialism of any type leads to a total destruction of the human spirit." It's painful to watch my country still being influenced by communist and socialist principles. These ideologies killed the Moldovan spirit and faith; citizens feel there is no hope for the future, either for themselves or Moldova. This is one of the reasons why the notion of socialism in the United States gives me such awful chills.

My parents, grandparents, and I all experienced what socialism is, and we can tell you, from first-hand experience, it is truly a terrible idea. Despite the slick, persuasive selling pitch U.S. politicians use to try to convince the American people otherwise, it never has been, never will be, and never can be. If you don't want to believe me and refuse to look at my country or the Soviet Union as an example of failure, mass death, and corruption, then consider looking into Venezuela in the year 2020. Venezuela has the largest reserves of crude oil in the world, yet it is completely in ruins. The crises of inflation, devalued currency, food shortages and famine, deficiency of medicine and potable water, electricity black outs (I remember them in the USSR and I am sure most Californians are familiar with the yearly, summer black outs as well...), high crime rate, and starvation have forced the productive class to escape Venezuela over the past 20 years. This is the kind of socialism some politicians in America aim to import to the U.S. Even though they gloss over the political agenda and will never admit to outright communism, the writing is on the wall. It's not difficult to see it, especially when you know how socialism smells, tastes, and feels.

Recently, I had an argument with one of my closest friends about socialism and how some politicians are trying to sell it to the greater U.S. population. His argument was that socialism is a good ideology for the U.S. "Look at Scandinavian countries," he says. It was so funny I laughed out loud a little. That is how this terrible ideology is packaged for the American people; "see how wonderful socialism works, look at Scandinavia they live so well... free education, free medical care, good pensions... blah, blah, blah." First of all, these Scandinavian states are not really socialist at their core. Secondly, nothing is free in this world – somewhere, somehow, someone is paying for the stuff we get for "free." In Scandinavian countries the idea is EVERYONE MUST PAY! Scandinavian countries do not target the rich or the one percent, they instead target the entire society. The entire population is responsible for not just healthcare, but also education and paid leave, meaning higher taxes across the board. It's a bucket where everyone contributes equally. As Jeffrey Dorfman writes, "the Nordic countries are smart enough not to kill the goose that lays the golden eggs." Contrary to the proponents of socialism in America, the Scandinavian countries don't deprecate corporations or the rich. They actually have lower corporate tax rates compared to the United States: 20 percent in Finland, 22 percent in Denmark and Sweden, and 23 percent in Norway. So, are the Scandinavian countries capitalist or socialist? Dinesh D'Souza sums it up best in his book, *The United States of Socialism*. "Scandinavians are capitalist in wealth creation and socialist in wealth distribution."

Lesson Learned: A socialism where everyone pays for the few who can't (or won't) work, is not self-sustaining.

Out of the Frying Pan; Into the Fire

The interesting thing emigrating from Moldova to the United States was getting away from a socialist society and venturing into a capitalist one. Even before I went to school for my undergraduate degree, I knew I wanted to move somewhere else and the United States was at the top of that list; from movies to TV shows to books, I saw America as the land of opportunities. Opportunities that I couldn't have even dared to dream of in Moldova, regardless of how much I studied or worked.

A push towards moving to America came from stories told to me by my cousin, Elena, and her husband, Shefic, who moved to the U.S. a full decade before myself. I was in my first year of college when Elena visited my parents, her Godparents, from the United States. And as Moldovans are known for hospitality, my mom prepared a feast for their arrival. We were all sitting at the table, drinking, eating,

America - The Architect of My Destiny

telling each other great stories about life - it was fabulous! Of course, everyone was intrigued by what my cousin and her husband thought about America and American culture. Shefic started on his observations. "I arrived in America with $450, with a student visa, not having a job or a home. Elena barely spoke English when she arrived in the U.S., but in the first couple of years, we were able to get a home and a car while going to school and working two jobs." Everyone at the table was shocked! My cousin continued. "I learned English and now I am studying to be a nurse practitioner." By the way, she finished top of her class, despite English not being her native language. My dad was curious and asked: "How were you able to achieve all of this?" Shefic responded. "You can do and be anything in America, you just have to have the desire to do so."

As I was listening, my mind began brainstorming how I could get to this amazing country. My cousin and her husband underwent a fairly easy process to get their student visas, due to Shefic being a Turkish citizen and his brother already being in the United States. In my case, while the chance to get any type of visa was very low, it was not altogether impossible. So, I began inquiring about how to get a visa to the United States. As my mother says, "if something gets to your head, nothing will stop you." She knows her daughter well!

I had heard of a program in my university called "Work and Travel." This program was specifically designed for students who wanted to work and travel in the United States or United Kingdom. It provided students with a way to visit the U.S. by helping them to work and earn spending money, whilst making friends from around the world and learning about the U.S. and its culture. The program placed international university students in temporary seasonal jobs throughout the U.S. for a three-month period. They had a few requirements; you had to be a full-time student between the ages of 18 and 28, able to work for a minimum of three months, and proficient in written and spoken English. There were also monetary requirements. The program itself cost $2,200. Not cheap for Moldova but it was my best chance to experience the United States. So how would I tell my parents I need $2,200 to pay for this program? I had to make a good case for them to even consider coming up with this amount of money. To build the case for my parents, I went to the agency offering the program. I inquired about the details; what are the chances of getting the visa? What are the requirements for the interviews with U.S. companies? And, most importantly, how much money can I earn in three months? They answered my questions, and my conclusion was that I had to go, no matter what!

During those times, my dad's business was struggling. I was not sure my parents would have $2,200 to finance me for this kind of trip, but I had to try. I spoke to my dad, explaining why I would like to go to the U.S. and what the benefits were. First, I told him that the $2,200 was a loan, not a giveaway. I would work during the summer and save to pay him back. Then, I told him that I would work hard to save enough money to pay for my last year of undergraduate studies. My dad was listening to me with a smile on his face, I'm sure thinking, "what in the world is she talking about?" That was a lot of money to save in three months. Dad told me he would be able to gather $1,700, but we need to brainstorm where to get the remainder. I thought about my cousin, Yuri; he might help; and, sure enough, he did. I am grateful to this day for the help he provided me 14 years ago. Once I got the okay from my dad and cousin, I started the process which would eventually lead me to where I am today.

Lesson Learned: Don't let obstacles stop you: rather, use them as motivation to achieve your goals.

The Interview With The Americans

The Work and Travel USA program is one facilitated by the U.S. government, allowing foreign university students to travel and work within the United States for several months. Run, more specifically, by the U.S. Department of State, the program has approximately 100,000 participants between the ages of 18 and 30 every year. Each student is sponsored by an American employer, and participants are issued a J-1 visa, a very rigorous process. Besides the requirements mentioned above, one has to pass multiple rounds of interviews with their U.S. employer and, most importantly, with the U.S. embassy in Moldova in order to obtain the J-1 visa to even travel to America. Before any of that is conducted, an application must be submitted alongside a $1,100 upfront fee. Once the application is submitted, a screening interview is scheduled with the U.S. program's staff to discuss job offers and options. I remember my interview with the U.S. representative like it was yesterday. I was very nervous! My English was weak so that added to my nervousness, but I wanted to go so badly. As I walked into the conference room, there were two ladies at a table with a sign that read "Texas, Omni Hotel." Next to them was another table with a sign for a restaurant chain in Alaska. Two different states with nearly 3,000 miles between them – two very different adventures. So together with my childhood friend, George (the only reason my dad allowed me to travel to another side of the world), we decided to start with Alaska, even though my heart was already set on Texas. We spoke to the Alaskan representative, or so we thought; who knows what they thought of our broken English. The job offer was for a restaurant chain as a cashier making $6.50 an hour. It was pretty tempting for two Moldovan students, but I didn't want to go to Alaska. It felt like going to a different part of Russia, not the U.S. We thanked them and moved on to the table with the Texas sign, my favorite.

The two ladies spoke with heavy southern accents we could barely understand. My friend and I had to concentrate hard to comprehend their words. Despite not being able to fully understand, I loved their warm, southern accents and open personalities. It felt very familiar to me, as if I had known them for a while. From what we could gather, it was the better paying job with the added potential for overtime. The job was a bit more complex and not what I was hoping to do in the U.S., but I didn't mind hard work for a shot at Texas. It was a housekeeping job at the Omni Hotel in Corpus Christi for $7.25 an hour, plus the opportunity for double that if overtime was available. We were sold. I was not afraid of work; after all it's what my parents did and taught me my whole life. Never be afraid or embarrassed to do a decent job!

I didn't know anything about Corpus Christi other than it's on the coast of the Gulf of Mexico. I had never seen the ocean in my life, so I was excited, but ultimately, all that mattered was that I was going to Texas! I mean cowboys, boots, Dallas, J.R. Ewing, everything I wanted to see since I first saw the show *Dallas*. We signed the job offer!

The next, and most important step was the interview with the U.S. ambassador. This was the U.S. government deciding if we qualified to travel to America. It makes complete sense; they want the best people to come and work in their country. But, I was at their mercy. Before the interview, we had an orientation with a Moldovan company that taught us how to behave during the interview – the do's and don'ts. We were somewhat aware and prepared for the interview, but nothing can fully prepare you for an interview with the U. S. government - it's intimidating! I got inside the embassy and took my seat, waiting for my name to be called. Once it was, I went inside the cabin where I faced the U. S. ambassador. There was a big glass window that separated us from one another. The ambassador was a tall man, mid 40's. He looked up, smiled, and welcomed me. I was glad to see his smile; it broke the ice. He asked me to introduce myself in English, which I did well. After all, I had been learning how to introduce myself in English since I was in 5th grade. Next, he asked me why I wanted to travel to the U.S. and why, specifically, Texas. I was well prepared for this question. I offered him a small smile and replied in English: "I always dreamed of visiting the U.S. since I was in second grade, especially Texas. I used to watch the show *Dallas*." He started to smile when I said *Dallas*, I guess he was familiar with the show. I continued. "I love the countryside, ranches, cowboys and boots, I think it's a beautiful state." My answer elicited a pleasant smile on his face, which made me feel slightly more confident. "Wonderful!" He said. "I wish you good luck on your travels to Texas." He held onto my passport and I knew right then I had gotten the J-1 visa to the U.S. I knew if the ambassador didn't return the passport it was a great sign. I was overjoyed. I called my dad right away. "Let's get my luggage ready; I am going to Texas." This moment determined my future. A future I am still, to this day, so grateful for.

Lesson Learned: This dream couldn't have been realized, were it not for the generosity of the U.S. Department of State "Work and Travel USA" program.

Chapter 3

Branching Out

"It always seems impossible until it is done."
- Nelson Mandela

America, Here I Come

The United States is, undoubtedly, one of the most forejudged countries in the world, both for positive and negative reasons. That is why most of the exchange students, myself included, already had a lot of preconceived stereotypes before arriving in the U.S. This can be primarily attributed to the tremendous influence of American pop culture all over the world; from Hollywood movies and music, to the influence of social media. Due to the fact that America is the most popular country for exchange students, there was always talk about their experiences.

    When I arrived in Corpus Christi, Texas, the first thing I noticed was the big trucks in the parking lots and streets. It seemed the bigger the car, the more presence you had on the road. I loved the big pickup trucks; I thought it was so cool. I learned early on that having a car in the U.S. is a must! If you don't have a car, you need someone to drive you or public transportation will become your best friend.

Another thing I observed in the first few days was just how talkative and friendly people were. I had never before experienced a complete stranger stopping to say hello and ask how I was doing; it was eye opening.

George and I were not the only Moldovan exchange students, there were another 20 or so with us. They all came from different parts of Moldova, but most of them were students from Chisinau Universities. We had a program coordinator called Darlene. She was a tall, American Canadian lady with a kind heart and a brilliant personality; you could hear her laugh throughout the whole of the hotel and instantly know who it was.

After we arrived, we were distributed into different apartments with four students in each. I was in a one-bedroom apartment with three other girls, never having met them before in my life. Two were sleeping in the bedroom and two in the living room. The apartment complex was called "Paradise Bay," which you would think, by the name, would match the reputation of the place, but to our chagrin it did not. We didn't realize until later on that "Paradise Bay" was in fact "Abyss Bay." The first time I was enlightened about the building's reputation was one evening when my American coworker gave me a ride home. Her boyfriend was driving and asked me where they should take me. When I said "Paradise Bay," they both looked at me with solemn faces, as if I had said "Hell Bay." My coworker replied, "It's not a good place; make sure you do not walk alone at night around there." In addition to the not so great living arrangements, I developed a terrible skin allergy within the first two weeks of arriving. I was terrified. My body was covered with red dots, itchy and uncomfortable.

I didn't know what to do or where to go, and generally felt hopeless. I mean where does an international student go, when they barely speak English, don't have a car, and don't know how to find a doctor? Thank God for Darlene. As soon as I told her she took me to a skin specialist. The doctor checked me out and determined it was reactions to the food, due to changes in my environment and nutrition. He prescribed some medication, which I had to put on daily. My poor roommates, Tanea and Lilia, had to help me apply it after a long day of housekeeping. It was not fun! I could not even go to the beach and enjoy the ocean. Fortunately, though, after three weeks, the allergies went away, and I was able to enjoy the sun and Corpus Christi's beaches once more.

Lesson Learned: The appreciation of other cultures and traditions.

Housekeeping

Let me be frank - housekeeping is hard work and I don't particularly like it. It's a demanding job, both mentally and physically. Does anyone actually "like" doing chores? Unless, of course, you are OCD. When I first signed on to the job, I knew I would be doing housekeeping in a big hotel with hundreds of rooms, so it wasn't a surprise by any means. The first day on the job we had an orientation with the housekeeping supervisor. He explained to us that a housekeeping job is not something to take lightly. He noted that the outcome of our tasks are directly responsible, to a great extent, for the hotel's reputation. Hence, there are strict requirements for the cleanliness and tidiness of each task that each housekeeper must implement thoroughly. These tasks include wiping down the bathtub and toilet; dusting all the glass doors, windows, mirror, and TV; emptying the trash can; refilling the minibar and tea set; and hoovering and mopping the floors and floorboards. I was familiar with my duties since reading the contract, so I was expecting the hard work.

What I was not expecting was the extreme pressure. The Omni Hotel had a requirement that each room be turned over in about 17 minutes. This means the housekeeper usually must rush through, on average, 20–25 rooms per day to ensure they are ready for customers come check-in. During the summer there were so many new guests checking in each day that the housekeepers not only had to follow the right procedures but also finish their tasks that much faster. Many rooms required more time and energy to clean than others, Sundays and Mondays being the worst for me. They're not only the days with the most check-outs, but they also result in rooms which are the aftermath of wild, weekend parties beyond imagination. I can't begin to describe the horrors I uncovered in some of these rooms.

Besides my housekeeping job, I had a second job in the hotel restaurant as a hostess. The restaurant manager, Robert, hired me primarily because I fit the type of worker he needed for that role; a young, pretty girl capable of speaking a few languages - the perfect hostess for a five-star restaurant. I worked in the restaurant from 5pm-11pm, Friday through Sunday, and it was a wonderful job I enjoyed very much. The restaurant was located on the 20th floor with an incredible view overlooking the water.

The menu and guests were exquisite. It's not a cheap place by Corpus Christi standards.

When I started the job I was so lost. I didn't know anything about being a hostess. However, God placed on my path many wonderful people like my dear friend, Monica. She was patient and taught me everything; from booking guests to seating them at the table. Indeed, I met a lot of wonderful people during my three months in Texas.

Having two jobs was not a piece of cake. Oftentimes I would have 10-15 check-outs on top of 8-10 check-ins in one day. The most difficult day for me was Sunday, because I had to finish cleaning all the rooms by 5pm to be able to go straight to my second job. My friend, Valeria, usually worked on the same floor as me or a floor below. On Sundays, I used to implore her for help. "Valeria, please, just change and make three beds for me that will help me tremendously." She never hesitated to pitch in. I ran around like a chicken with its head cut off for the whole three months.

There were two things I hated about housekeeping; the heavy, metal cart we all had to push around and the vacuuming. This cart was heavy for a skinny 20-year-old girl with little arms to push around. It was filled with everything a housekeeper needed to clean the rooms; clean sheets, towels, shampoo and conditioner, and the vacuum. The dreaded vacuum. Because it was a heavy, industrial grade vacuum, it was difficult to work with and lug around, especially 15 times a day. I made sure I told my husband well before we got married that I detest vacuuming due to my experience as a housekeeper. He laughed and said, "I guess I will be vacuuming all my life now."

A funny story I often laugh with my exchange program friends about is the cart on my leg. I was always in a hurry to finish my housekeeping duties so I could get to my second job. One Friday, as I was lugging the vacuum on my back and scrambling with the cart around a corner, it began toppling over and my lumbering attempts to prevent catastrophe brought me directly under the thing, trapped by my leg.

So there I am, stuck with a vacuum on my back and a heavy cart on my leg, pinned in the middle of the hotel floor. With guests in their rooms, I didn't want to scream and make a fuss, so that left me with few options. Luckily, one of my friends was on the same floor as me, so I called for her with desperation in my voice. She came and helped lift the cart enough to let me wriggle my way out. Then she had to find some other girls, while I recovered my composure, to help us right the cart back onto its wheels and collect the bits and pieces that had scattered. I was late for my shift in the restaurant that night, but the big bruise on my thigh and slighted look told my supervisor I had a legitimate excuse. Now you know why I hated that damn cart and vacuuming so much!

Housekeeping is certainly not an easy job, nor a glamorous one. Between waking up early in the morning, vacuuming 15-25 rooms a day and cleaning nasty bathrooms and dirty sheets you are exhausted by the end of the day. Despite these realities, it was, undoubtedly, the most important job I had in my life. It taught me a great lesson, humility. Even though I had travelled half-way around the world, had almost attained my undergraduate degree, and spoke four languages, I still conducted my job gratefully and humbly.

Humility is the secret sauce in the recipe of success, no matter what you do in life, whether you experience success or setbacks. We are all human after all, and therefore flawed and vulnerable in our own unique ways. And self-awareness is paramount to the cultivation of humility. I knew deep down that this was not the end for me, but rather the beginning. I was performing my housekeeping duties with gratitude and diligence, knowing that the opportunities going forward were endless.

Lesson Learned: Don't be afraid of hard work, be proud. It will pay off eventually.

The Opportunity

Despite some difficulties, coming to the U.S. was the best thing that happened to me. I absolutely loved the experience and cherished the opportunity presented. You need to understand, I come from a country where opportunities are not easy to come by. There is no "Moldovan dream" or "land of opportunity;" and, if an opportunity magically arises, you take advantage of it no matter the circumstances. It's like someone telling you: "there is a door, the only door, and no matter what you do you have to go through that door." Failure is not an option either. If you fail once, you might never get an opportunity again. Like when I was a child, if we were not in line for bread by 6:15 sharp each morning, the opportunity to get bread passed us by for the day.

In the United States of America, the land of opportunity and American dream are tangible. It's real, there is no need to search too far because it's right in front of you. I felt that as soon as I arrived in the U.S. I don't know how you can miss it unless you don't want to see it. Imagine, a little girl from a country that no one has ever heard of was able to get two jobs and make almost $5,500 in three months. I was only 20 years old with broken English, but that didn't stop me. It didn't prevent me from succeeding. I was able to buy my first laptop, camera, and a bunch of other material items and still have $3,500 remaining to pay back my dad and cousin. Maybe that's not a lot of money for an American citizen, but for a young Moldovan girl it was a significant amount. Besides earning a decent amount of money, I made some amazing friends, connections, and timeless memories. Some friendships continue to this day, such as my maid of honor and dear friend, Cristina. I met her in 2007 and we've maintained a friendship for the past 14 years. In fact, I am her son's godmother. Another lifetime friendship and sisterhood is my American friend, Christina. She and her family are massive contributors to who I am today. She was my savior when I was in desperate need. More about her later.

At the end of summer, we had to return to Moldova. I felt quite downcast, and my only thoughts were on how to make it back to this wonderful country. However, I made a promise to myself and to my parents that I would finish my undergraduate degree before emigrating *anywhere*, so that was that. I definitely didn't want to disappoint my parents, who were paying for my tuition and had always dreamed of seeing me graduate. Nevertheless, I knew I wanted to move to America as soon as I finished my degree; there was no doubt in my mind that the country was my future. Once I arrived back in Moldova, I began my last year of college. Besides being able to pay for my final year outright, I was able to return $2,000 to my parents. I was so proud of myself. I was following my parents lead in becoming independent and responsible. My mom could not believe I was capable of earning so much money in such a short amount of time. She said, "you could never accomplish such a thing in Moldova."

My last year in college was slightly less challenging due to my having less classes to focus on my thesis. A byproduct of this was that it gave me more free time, so I got a part time job as an accountant for my cousin's furniture company. I was making $100 a month, which was not a lot of money but enough to save for my ticket to the U.S. I was very determined to get back there, so much so that my stubbornness made my mom a bit nervous. She could not understand why I was so eager to leave my family and friends to move to a different country, on a different continent, all alone and not knowing exactly where I would end up and who I would know there. She used to say, "what did the Americans do to you?" My poor mom; no matter how old you get, moms never stop being moms. I knew America was where I wanted to build my future. Somehow, I knew that there was no country in the world like it. I was attracted to the mixture of freedom, patriotism, liberty, opportunity, things that I still, to this day, have yet to encounter elsewhere. That's the spirit of America. As poet Ralph Waldo Emerson once said, "America is another name for opportunity. Our whole history appears like a last effort of divine providence on behalf of the human race."

Lesson Learned: Decide what you want in life and go for It.

Goodbye Moldova

I love my native country, despite its weaknesses. Moldova was never an economic or political powerhouse. It doesn't have any influence on the international stage. It's considered one of the poorest countries in Europe. It is beggarly, particularly economically and politically; but not spiritually or traditionally. From the beautiful history of wine making, pottery, ceramics, and crafts, to traditional embroideries and Doina music (traditional Romanian music style), Moldova has many wonderful traditions.

My compatriots are wonderful people with an immense heart for hospitality. You never walk away hungry from a Moldovan household; serving the best dishes to your guests is a-must! One of the qualities I admire and dislike all at the same time is overworking. Yes, there is such a thing in my country as working too hard. When I say too hard, I mean in vain without much progress or hope for a better future. The main reason for this state of being is the loss of hope. If you talk to different people in different professions about their happiness and quality of life, you would likely draw one conclusion: Moldovan people are unhappy as a result of their lack of hope. Hope is the only thing stronger than fear.

Moldovan people are fearful of what tomorrow might bring; uncertainties, hardships, despair. The lack of hope in Moldova is rooted in our culture. I remember reading an article in the *Wall Street Journal* from 2009 titled, "The World's Most Unhappy People." The article was based on research done by Eric Weiner, "The Geography of Bliss." The author's year-long search for the world's unhappiest place led him to Moldova. Weiner cites Moldovans lack of a solid sense of identity, pride of nation, and hope for the future as their main reasons for unhappiness. That, along with grinding poverty and corruption, help explain why as many as one-quarter of all Moldovans emigrate and work abroad, sending back the remittances that keep the country afloat.

Moldova is a country lost within its own corruption. In 2014, $1 billion disappeared from three national banks. The fraud cost Moldovan taxpayers the equivalent of 12 percent of the GDP, which, for a Moldovan, is a significant amount.

The bank fraud in Moldova was a coordinated effort, involving high level officials in collusion with select bankers in all three banks to extract as much "borrowed" capital as possible without any apparent rationale. Fund's worth $1 billion dollars were transferred to United Kingdom and Hong Kong shell companies in order to conceal the real owners of the underlying assets. After the investigation and prosecution was complete, only a few of them took the fall and went to jail, the "big dogs" running away to European countries. Now, they are living in their mansions in London, Geneva, and Turkey; whereas, the Moldovan people are living in destitution. That's why people don't have hope in the future of Moldova; with such a government, who would.

I know there is corruption everywhere in the world, even in America, but nowhere is quite like Moldova. Favoritism and nepotism are normal governmental occurrences. They will participate in a scheme to defraud their country, only to backstab each other or flee to non-extradition countries.

I was very familiar with that internal, deep seeded unhappiness. I saw it everywhere. I saw it in my parents, friends, teachers, and especially the younger generation. The youth understood this reality well; there was no hope for the future. I saw it too and I knew that if I wanted a better future for myself, I had to leave behind everything I knew, everything I had, and everything I held dear in my beloved country. There was no other way.

Lesson Learned: Moldova is my soul; the United States of America is the architect of my dreams.

Welcome Back, Sweetheart!

When I first came to the U.S., I felt a sense of identity, pride, patriotism… hope. Something I was not experiencing in my native country. As I approached my graduation in May of 2008, I was set in stone on moving to America. I knew the magnitude of my decision and the consequences it might incur; but I also knew nothing was going to stop me.

America - The Architect of My Destiny

The most difficult part of this decision was moving so far away from my family. My parents understood I had a vision for my life and that, until I achieved it, I would feel restless. They knew it was fruitless to try and convince me otherwise; I was ready to take the risk and move across the world by myself. My parents also knew they had prepared me for this journey, providing me with the right tools to embark on this adventure without hesitation. They instilled in me the core values, principles, and morals that influence all my behaviors and attitudes which affect my daily decisions and relationships. All that I am I owe to my parents. I can say without a shadow of a doubt that they've been the biggest blessing in my life up until the day I married my husband. Sitting here writing about them gives me a kind of "stage fright," because I can't quite seem to come up with the words to explain just how much I love and cherish them.

After I finished my exams and submitted my graduation thesis, I was ready to move to the U.S. I managed to get a work contract via my previous employer in the restaurant, which included decent pay and a housing allowance for 3 months. I could not be happier, because it meant I had a solid case for the U.S. ambassador to grant me a working visa. Indeed, it did; I was granted the visa that same May, and by June 27th I was on a flight to Houston, Texas. This moment, right here, was where my challenging, inspiring, and amazing journey began. It is the moment I started living the American dream. I had one suitcase full of dreams and 100 dollars in my pocket, ready to conquer the greatest country in the world.

Lesson Learned: Never forget the people in your life who contributed to your success.

The Sweet Beginning

I'm sure you're thinking what most of my friends wondered. "How did you survive with just 100 dollars for the first month?" Well I did, and I had approximately 20 dollars left before I got my first paycheck. The idea of saving and being frugal in order to survive was nothing new. My parents were forced to learn this skill during Soviet times and knew how important it would be for my brother and I." You never know what situation you might end up in in life, therefore, you better know how to be economical." They were so right! While working in the restaurant I was also looking for a second job to improve my financial situation.

It was not easy to find a job, however, due to the economic crash of 2008. I was approaching the end of my contract with the restaurant, which meant I was about to lose my job and my housing, and I didn't have anyone to rely on. There was no help, or so I thought, until I met my "saving angel" and sister from another mother, Christina.

Christina was also working at the restaurant as a waitress and heard about my situation from the restaurant manager. She heard I was approaching joblessness and homelessness with no family to help. This is where God intervened; He didn't let me despair or lose hope, and He put Christina on my path. Christina approached me with a job offer about a week before my contract expired at the restaurant; and it was by no means a simple offer. It was an offer to become part of her wonderful and loving family. She proposed that

I babysit her two twin boys and her eight-year-old daughter, as well as live with them as part of the family. She provided me with my own room, a car, free rent, and 8 dollars an hour for my babysitting. Moreover, she provided me with a family! I could not believe that a complete stranger could be so kind to another complete stranger.

She didn't owe me anything. I was nothing to her but she helped me without a second thought, and for that I will be forever grateful. Christina is a perfect example of the American spirit, especially in Texas. The kind of selfless and loving spirit that's ready to help a stranger at a moment's notice. During almost 14 years in the U.S I met a ton of amazing people, from different cultures and walks of life, and they all contributed to my journey one way or another. I will always remember them for everything they did for me.

I lived and worked with Christina for six happy months before deciding to move to Galveston, Texas. I wanted more for my life than babysitting, so I knew I needed to move to a bigger city with more opportunities. I originally wanted to move to Houston and enroll in a graduate program, but unfortunately I didn't have the means just yet. Galveston was close enough to Houston for me to transfer later on, when I had advanced my finances.

I had a school friend from Moldova living in Galveston at the time, who was able to help me with housing and securing a job. He lived in a 2-bedroom apartment with four of his friends, making me the sixth roommate. I didn't complain about how overcrowded the place was, as I was just happy to have a roof over my head and a job to provide for myself. The job I found was at the Hilton, working as a waitress for the breakfast rush. My morning shift started at 6am, and in order for me to be on time I had to leave my apartment at 5am. It was a bit of a hike, at just over 2 miles walking, but I didn't have a car so it was my only option. I remember walking down the seawall in the early morning darkness, paralyzed by the howling wind and rain. Oftentimes I would arrive at work soaking wet, red in the face from battling the seawall gales; however, all that mattered was that I had a job and a way to start saving money to pay for my master's degree.

You see, I had a basic goal in mind: work hard at 2-3 jobs and save the majority of my money for tuition. I didn't want to take student loans; the thought of owing money to the government scared me. I still had a thorn in my side when it came to owing *anything* to the government. I believed (and still do to this day) that if you owe anything to the government, the government in turn owns you. This lesson came direct from my childhood as well as the stories my parents and grandparents passed down. No one in my country trusts the government; they are all scared that the government would come and confiscate everything they've worked so hard for.

That's what the socialist and communist government did to our people for years. They were left starving with no hope for tomorrow. My grandmother absolutely despises the government, especially the banking system. She and Grandpa worked all their lives to save a few thousands rubles in order to help their kids when they started their own families. When the Soviet Union collapsed, the financial system crashed causing massive currency devaluation. Their five thousand rubles was reduced to fifty rubles overnight, and it was absolutely devastating. Thankfully my grandparents weren't in debt to the government, or they would have lost their land and home too. It was such a traumatic blow that some people committed suicide over the reality of losing their life savings, and all their belongings to the government. Time doesn't necessarily heal all wounds, especially when it comes to trusting the government, nor should it. As my father always says, "trust is hard to gain and easy to lose."

My grandmother's wounds are so immense that she keeps her money under her pillow to this day... and why wouldn't she?! When the socialist/communist government can come in at any time and take everything you've worked so hard for, the notion of 'trust' becomes irrelevant. When she first heard that I was going to school for finance and banking, she asked my dad, "did you send her to school so she can learn how to cheat people out of their money?" She definitely did not like my choice of school faculty. Even though I experienced less disappointment with the banking system and government, I too, did not like the idea of owing anything to anyone. As I got familiar with the school system in the U.S., I understood the consequences of school loans. I didn't want to be paying school loans well into my old age, so saving and paying for my education was not a choice, it was a must!

Lesson Learned: New beginnings are scary, unpredictable, and uncomfortable but so necessary for our development.

I Got Wheels

I can definitely say that the first couple of years in the U.S. were the most difficult ones. Difficult for many reasons - financially, mentally, physically. At one point, I was barely making ends meet. For a couple of weeks, rice and ramen noodles were all I could afford to eat. Yes, I could call my parents and ask them for help, but for me that would have meant admitting defeat. Defeat in the sense of not being able to apply all the knowledge and education my parents imbued me with in order to succeed. They provided me with all the tools I needed to live "The American Dream"; I just had to put it into action. The most important thing I had to remember was no matter how many times I failed, I had to get up and try again, and again, until I triumphed. Failure was not an option; you never give up despite the difficulties you encounter on the journey.

I knew I needed to improve my financial situation, and for that I needed a vehicle. The bike I purchased a few months prior met a bad fate and was stolen, so I decided to vigorously save all my money to purchase a small, cheap vehicle. With the help of a friend, I was able to find a 2000 Ford Focus Coupe on Craigslist for roughly $3,350 dollars. We went to meet the seller, a nice lady in her mid 40s, and check out the car; it was in very good condition but I only had $3,250 saved up at that point. I told her I was $100 short and asked if she could lower the price a notch so I could afford it. She looked at me with a smile on her face. "I will give you the car for $3,200 and give you $20 for gasoline." I could not believe it - I had just bought my own car with my own, hard earned money!

When I sat in my car for the first time, I felt so proud. I mean, I *owned* that car. When you save and pay for something yourself, you just treat it differently, you have a greater appreciation for it. I immediately called my parents to share the wonderful news. They could not believe that their baby girl was able to move across the globe, work hard, and buy her first car; it was a proud moment for all of us. This was the moment when I realized everything, and anything is possible in the U.S. if you have the desire, and the will.

The American system is created for everyone to take advantage of it. The capitalist system is built in such a way that it allows regular individuals to acquire and own private property, and use the free market to create wealth. This is one of the reasons I love America so much. The lack of government intervention, means of production owned by private firms, and goods and services distributed according to price mechanisms (as opposed to government price controls) makes the system profitable and efficient. Capitalism is about innovation as much as it is invention. One of the great essays in the free-market tradition is Leonard Read's "I, Pencil." Read was the founder of the influential American think tank, Foundation for Economic Education. In his essay, he adopts the perspective of an ordinary, wooden pencil and purports to track his genealogy. He begins as a cedar tree from Northern California or Oregon, is chopped down, harvested, and shipped by train to a mill in San Leandro, California, where he is then refined to "small, pencil-length slats less than one fourth of an inch in thickness." Read's point? Not a single person on the face of this earth knows how to make a pencil on their own. The construction of a pencil is dispersed among "millions of human beings," from the Italians who mine pumice for the eraser, to the coffee manufacturers who supply drinks to the cedar loggers in Oregon. That's capitalism - the engine that drives economic growth, creativity, and opportunity for all.

I often hear the complaint from capitalism "haters" that capitalism is not fair and doesn't provide equal opportunities for everyone – I think this is nonsense. Yes, capitalism is sometimes not fair or perfect, but it is a good system. A fair society ensures that its members have equality of opportunities, not equality of outcomes, as mandated by anti-capitalists. The outcome is your responsibility and yours alone. Each one of us has the same opportunity that Jeff Bezos did to start a business (Amazon) selling books from his garage and potentially become a trillionaire. Jeff Bezos didn't come from a wealthy family; he is an ordinary man with a keen instinct for seizing opportunities, and blessed to grow up in the free market system of the United States of America.

History shows that socialism promises prosperity, equality, and security, but in actuality delivers poverty, misery, and tyranny. It drives governmental control, the destruction of human freedom, and an artificial equality in every example, bar none, of its execution. Yes, equality is achieved for the majority, in the sense that almost everyone is equal in their capacity for misery.

When Vladimir Lenin took power in Russia in 1917, he promised: "land for the peasants, peace to the nation, and bread for the starving." He did provide land to the peasants, by redistributing land from wealthy farmers, but within a year the new farmers were forced to give up their entire surplus of products to the government. What followed was known as the "man-made famine." History clearly shows that the difference between capitalism and socialism is that capitalism works, for the most part (so long as corruption is stifled), whereas socialism fails every time (due to corruption). As Aleksandr Solzhenitsyn once wrote, "socialism of any type leads to total destruction of the human spirit and to a leveling of mankind into death... socialism cannot be implemented without the aid of coercion."

We have better standards of living than our ancestors because of the little things we created over the years, because of innovation; and, there is no innovation without the presence of a free market, or capitalism.

Once I bought a car, my commute became easier and freer. I was on the lookout for a second job when one day, I went by my bank to deposit my paycheck. Right there, in front of the teller desk, was a hiring sign that peaked my interest. After all, I did graduate from the Academy of Economics with a degree in finance and banking; this was a perfect job for me. I started conversing with the teller and told her about my interest in the position; she asked me to complete an application and wait for a call. Two days later, a call came from the branch manager who wanted to schedule an interview with me. I could not believe it! How could they be interested in a Moldovan girl with a rough accent and no experience in banking?! Later on, I understood that in the U.S., it doesn't matter whether or not you have an accent, where you come from, or what your background is; what matters is how you persevere and persist to achieve your goal. The environment is seeded with opportunities that are there for you to explore and take advantage of. After two interviews, my journey into the banking industry began!

Lesson Learned: In a capitalist society anyone can succeed, you just must have the desire to do so.

The Bank on the Corner of the Street

My first job at the bank was working as a teller for IBC, a local Texas bank. What I liked most about the company was their training process. For a month, I was sent to the headquarters in Houston to undergo a rigorous training program. The structure was similar to a college class with special instructors, learning materials, and exams. If you didn't pass the final exam, you couldn't work in the bank. Reflecting back on this experience, I realize how advantageous it was. Despite graduating with a degree in finance and banking, I was not familiar with the American banking industry. My knowledge of banking and finance was based on the European system, which has a lot of similarities but equally as many distinctions from the U.S. system. This experience served as a foundation for me in the industry, eventually leading me to improve going forward. I liked working at IBC Bank. It was a nice environment with great colleagues, but the pay was low; in fact, I believe it was the lowest paying bank during those times.

For a couple of years, I had my eye set on a different bank - Texas First Bank. Before I was able to purchase a car, I walked everywhere in Galveston. Once a week I would walk a mile with my friend to the laundromat to wash our clothes. On the way we would pass 61st Street, where construction of the new Texas First Bank branch was in full development. Every time we walked by I used to comment to my friend. "One day I am going to work there." He used to laugh at me, thinking I was dreaming too big , aspiring for too much. Nevertheless, I knew in my mind and heart my aspiration would come to fruition sooner or later.

I believe great discovery takes shape in the mind before it manifests physically. Likewise, our aspirations and dreams must first take root in our mind's eye. I utilize my imagination a lot! As Stephen Covey describes in his book, *The 7 Habits of Highly Effective People*, "the ability to envision in your mind what you cannot at present see with your eyes. It is based on the principle that all things are created twice. There is a mental (first) creation, and a physical (second) creation. The physical creation follows the mental, just as a building follows a blueprint..." We need to work on envisioning and compelling our futures. It might sound cliche but I have a vision board. It is comprised of all the goals and aspirations I would like to achieve in the near future. It provides me with a daily, visual reminder of my dreams and plans. Visualization is one of the most powerful mind exercises you can do. According to the popular book, *The Secret,* "the law of attraction is forming your entire life experience and it is doing that through your thoughts. When you are visualizing, you are emitting a powerful frequency out into the Universe." I know visualization works because it worked for me. Moreover, once I got married, my husband and I created our family vision board; it's a sacred space that displays what we want to achieve and bring to life. What we focus on expands.

Even when we face setbacks, that vision board is still there, ready to motivate us all over again.

My vision board, at this time, included working for the new Texas First Bank. I was visualizing for over a year and it was the time to put my dreams into action. One day I decided to go by the branch and introduce myself to the manager, Dianna. I thought to myself, what's the worst that can happen? She might say she doesn't have a position for me, but it doesn't matter; the answer will always be, no" until I ask. Dianna was an African American woman with a lovely smile and admirable attitude. A kind and respectful lady, she carefully listened to me, asked me a few questions, and eventually informed me that she didn't have an available position at the moment. I didn't despair, rather I thanked her and told her that I would check back soon. She didn't know me well enough back then to know that when I said soon, I meant every week. Yes, every week I would inquire about a position and leave with the same answer, until one day the answer I left with was yes. After a few week's worth of visits, she told me she was able to find me a part-time position as a teller. I was overjoyed by the news - my vision came to fruition. After a few months on the job, we were having our monthly one-on-one and she asked me a question. "Do you know why I offered you the job?" I replied. "No." She smiled at me and said, "in my 30 years of experience in the banking industry, I have never seen anyone want a job as much as you did. I could see in your eyes, the desire for hard work and I could not refuse you." Dianna is still a very close friend and mentor, and I am forever grateful for the opportunity she provided me with when I desired it the most.

Besides working in the bank during the week, I had a second job on the weekends as a cocktail waitress at Sharon's inside the Moody Gardens Hotel. I loved working there for multiple reasons; from making good tips to the piano player, Steve. Every Friday and Saturday night, Steve performed in the restaurant's lounge. The piano music helped the nights go by with a smile, despite feeling tired and overwhelmed. It was a small thing that helped me enjoy the job even more. The people I worked with were such an amazing crew. The guys in the kitchen knew I came to the restaurant directly from my shift at the bank, and they always made sure I was fed. Cedric, the kitchen chef, would prepare something small for me before the restaurant got busy and again before the night was over.

I mentioned I made good tips due to the contingent of guests that visited the restaurant. These were the elite of Galveston; distinguished guests that included the Moody family, the CEO of Galveston's biggest insurance company, as well as many of the local retired judges. Over time I learned how to make my well-deserved tips by observing my guests' individual and distinct preferences. I knew they appreciated an elevated kind of service, so I made them feel special either with the drink they liked at the perfect time, or with their favorite dessert after dinner.

I am a very detail-oriented person, and it served me well in my waitressing. This job taught me how to build the most relevant and hirable skills, preparing me even more for the "real world." I think anyone who has worked in the food service industry will agree, the job in and of itself is not always fun or easy but it offers an essential skill set for future career opportunities. Whilst being a waitress, I learned many valuable skills that I apply in my life and career every day. Skills such as customer service, multitasking, time management, patience, or being kind (even though you really don't want to). All these skills are extremely important, regardless of what field you end up in later on in life.

Lesson Learned: What we think, what we say, what we do, creates our reality.

Free Education

Working as a teller or a waitress in a restaurant might teach you great life skills, but there is not much advancement for the future – at least not the future I envisioned for myself. By this point in time, I had saved half of the sum I needed to sponsor my master's degree, but before that I needed some basic classes: ESL (English as a second or foreign language) and Government. I was still living in Galveston, and I heard a rumor from some coworkers that if you graduate high school in Galveston, you get two years of community college for free. It sounded too good to be true; I mean free education, I'd never heard of that before in my life. Where I come from nothing is free, you pay for your education, or you don't get one! As strange as it sounded, I decided to visit the Galveston community college to see if the rumor was legitimate. The student advisor confirmed it to be true and said that if any student graduates high school, they get two years of basic classes for free at Galveston Community College. I started to brainstorm right away.

The student advisor explained that I could take the GED (General Educational Development) which, if I passed, would place me in the category of "graduate of Galveston High School." "The exam fee is 60 dollars and we have preparation classes for the exam," she said. I was astonished. You can get a high school diploma with only 60 dollars to your name, plus free classes to prepare you for the exam??? Unbelievable!

I decided to register for the exam and free preparatory courses; after all, it was ONLY 60 dollars! I wasn't sure what the classes entailed or what to expect, but once I started it was clear to me that it was basic math, science, and English – that's it. I was confident about my aptitude for science and math, but English required a little bit of improvement. Our class was very diverse; we had Mexican, Salvadorian, Colombian, African American, Caucasian, Polish, Moldovan, and Kazakh (my friend, Anton) students. We were all there to get our GEDs and Anton and I were both in the same boat; children of the USSR, fluent in Russian and proficient in math and science, but English not so much. We both concentrated on English by learning grammar and writing essays. After three months I took the exam and passed with no issues. After all, I already had an undergraduate degree in Economics - I had to pass.

Ironically, I graduated high school twice; once in Moldova and once in the U.S. This situation again demonstrated to me that it's never too late to strive for your dreams. In my GED prep course I had people with different ages, from different walks of life, alongside me trying to improve their futures. It didn't matter what they did or didn't do 10 or 20 years ago, what mattered was that they were there, in that class, working towards their goals. In America, you're never too late or too old to go after your dreams. I remember seeing on TV an amazing case of a 98- year-old man getting his high school diploma. The man couldn't get his original diploma because he was drafted to fight in World War II. How inspiring is his story? If all this doesn't give you hope, I don't know what will.

Lesson Learned: It's never too late to start or finish something in life.

Chapter 4

THE FRUITS OF MY LABOR

"Success is no accident. It is hard work, perseverance, learning, studying, sacrifice and most of all, love of what you are doing or learning to do."
- Pele

No Success Without Failure

How do you define success? Is it money? Power? Higher education? What does success mean to you? These are questions we all ask ourselves at some point in time. Success, like happiness, is not a perpetuated stage, it descends upon you, every now and then. When it comes upon you, you should be grateful because, for all your success, there are plenty in the world still suffering. But, an important question arises: is there success without failure? And, how can you truly know what success is, if you've never experienced failure? After all, we all have failures in life. We all love to talk and brag about our successes but are very reluctant to recognize our failures. Failure is not something that most people welcome. Why would they? These are uncomfortable feelings that, as human beings, we tend to do our best to circumvent. Of one thing I am certain, there is no success without failure. In fact, failure is the secret ingredient to success. Without it, we will never be able to realize our full potential. Without failure, one does not understand what it means to succeed, since every action would just be seen as routine.

The former NFL quarterback, Chad Pennington, was interviewed for a book, "Raising Your Game: Over 100 Accomplished Athletes Help You Guide Your Girls and Boys Through Sports." When asked if there is success without failure, he responded, "you must go through some failures to get to where you want to go, whether it is in school or sports. We as parents have to focus on every once in a while letting our kids fail. We need to teach our kids not to accept failure, but to embrace failure and use it as a teaching experience, use it to learn from." Pennington's answers made me think about my parents.

I know that when I decided to move to the U.S., my parents considered I might fail in my endeavors. I remember sitting next to my dad just hours before my departure into the unknown world, he was lost in thought. A solemn look on his face and eyes filled with tears, he looked at me and said, "Honey, I can't stop you from embarking on this adventure, but never forget that you will always have a place to come back to and a family who loves you." To me, his words were giving me permission, moreover, encouraging me, to take the biggest risk of my life; and, if I failed, he and my family would be there to support and pick me back up. Of course, he believed in me and my abilities, but he didn't know what the outcome would be. What he did know was that his child needed to experience her adventure - and maybe a failure or two - before she could appreciate success. See, when you move out from under your parents protection into the real world, you don't win all the time. You don't get trophies every time you "play." It comes down to the journey you take, the effort you put in, and the things you learn along the way. When all is said and done, those milestones are more important than whether you succeed or fail.

I, like most people on this planet, have had my fair share of failures. Some have been small, like forgetting to call a friend on their birthday or running a stop sign, while others have been bigger, such as failing at my first marriage or hurting someone dear to me. We all have a collection of cry-in-my-teacup stories, yet the most important thing is that we don't let these failures define us. We should not allow our past to determine our future; rather, we need to acknowledge, accept, and embrace it. Life is going to take its course and there's nothing you can do to stop it, but you can control your attitude and reactions toward negative things. We may not be able to change the past, but we can change how we see it, the story we tell ourselves, and ultimately how it touches us and who we become. By altering our perspective, we can better envision a compelling future. I am my biggest critic. If I fail at something or make a mistake, I am my own judge, jury, and executioner. No one can judge me harsher than I can, but it's of no real benefit. Don't get me wrong, it's necessary to acknowledge your mistakes, take responsibility, and own them, but it's not advantageous to dwell on them and torture yourself long after they're in the rearview window.

Reliving my mistakes over and over again is like perpetually walking around with a bad haircut while pointing to my head and proclaiming, "look at what happened to me!"

Well, I decided to let it grow out! I understand that failures are precious life lessons which have to be learned, oftentimes the hard way. These lessons would not be learned if it was not for some failures and disappointments. I try to find the blessings contained within the curses of my past, and tell my story from a new perspective; because of that, I am able to see current and future challenges as opportunities. For me, in the end, success isn't what others tell me it is - it's what I say it is for myself!

Lesson Learned: Failure brings with it important, firsthand knowledge, and nothing can replace the knowledge gained from failure.

The Kid in the Candy Store

My biggest goal upon returning to the U.S. was to obtain my master's degree in business administration. It was something I had been working towards for the past two years at this point, preparing and saving money to pay for the tuition. It was 2014 when I was able to get a job with American National Insurance Company as an Accounting Specialist. It was a better job than any I had previously, with higher pay and better benefits. By this stage, I was living in the southern suburbs of Houston to be closer to work as well as to a college that I wanted to attend. I wanted to go to college, but I was not clear what steps I needed to take to get admitted. I didn't have many friends in my life to guide me through the process, so I started researching what I needed to do.

I knew I needed to receive accreditation for my Moldovan undergraduate degree in order to be on par with the U.S.

equivalent. I found an authority in Austin that was able to provide me with such accreditation. I wasn't entirely sure if I would receive full credit for all the classes I took in Moldova given that the U.S. education system is different from the Moldovan one. Luckily, I received more than enough credits (144 of a minimum 138) to be admitted for a master's degree. It was a blessing I was educated in banking and finance, as there is a ton of overlap with the U.S. field requirements. If I would have, for example, graduated with a degree in the legal field, I would have had to start from the beginning since the U.S. judicial system is so different from any European (certainly Eastern European) system.

I also needed to write a college admissions essay. I had no clue what such an essay. After a few days of researching, I understood the reason and value behind the essay. The college essay was my opportunity to highlight my best qualities and to show an admissions committee what makes me stand out from other applicants. I was very intimidated by such an idea. If writing is still my vulnerability six years removed, back then it could be best described as a paralyzing phobia. I was terrified and lost about what to write about in my essay. I didn't think I had any notable skills or an interesting background, so how could I stand out?

While brainstorming, I was casually talking to my coworker and told her about my dilemma. "I have nothing interesting to say in my essay." Amanda, my coworker, looked at me and rolled her eyes. She laughed. "You don't have anything interesting to write about? You must be kidding me! You, a 20-year-old girl, moved to another continent by yourself, barely speaking English, with a hundred dollars in her pocket, and you don't think that's interesting?" I looked at her confused, thinking to myself, no, not really. There are millions of people who did the same thing or even more, why should my story be considered interesting? She smiled at me and said something I will never forget. "It's interesting because it's your story." At that moment, a light bulb went on in my head. I realized I was comparing my life story against everyone else's, and in such competition I was "losing." I came to understand that I can only compete with myself, not with other people.

My story was interesting because it was my story and it was unique. In the end, I wrote an essay about my life not unlike this memoir. It was honest, raw, and transparent, detailing my all-consuming desire to study in the U.S. Of course, I asked Amanda to review my writing from a native English speaker's perspective, just to make sure my story made sense. She approved and I submitted the paperwork to three Texas universities. To my surprise, all three responded with a letter of acceptance, so I was once again blessed with the privilege of making a choice; I chose Texas Woman's University (TWU).

I picked TWU for a few reasons. First, the tuition was more affordable than the other two; second, their representatives were extremely helpful during my admissions period; and, last but not least, their program worked perfectly with my schedule. I was still able to be a full- time student, but with 50 percent on campus and 50 percent remote. It worked well for me since I still had a full-time job.

Have you ever observed a kid in the candy store? Their faces light up when they see all the candy they are about to enjoy. Well, that was my face on the first day of classes. I arrived 30 minutes early, "ready to rumble." I took my seat and sat there thinking about what my parents would think and feel about this. Would they be happy for me? Would they be proud? Then, as the students started to come in, another scary thought ran through my head – the thought that I might not be good enough to succeed. I thought about the prospect of facing embarrassment because of my poor English skills, or not being able to keep up with the rest of the students in class. All these crazy thoughts were racing through my head while the professor walked in and got ready to begin the lecture.

Mr. Werema was a professor of global business studies. A tall, middle-aged man from Kenya, he was very eloquent and had a soothing voice. He first introduced himself, recounting his immigration story and life in Kenya before coming to the U.S. It was quite an interesting tale; he, at one point, had experienced being kidnapped and held for ransom. Then, he asked us to introduce ourselves. There were many intriguing individuals with equally fascinating and diverse backgrounds. When the time came for me to introduce myself, I was sweating. I told everyone I was originally from Moldova, to which they all looked at me blankly, having never heard of the country. A few people were impressed by my multilingual skills, but to me it still felt like I was not good enough for the program.

After class, Mr. Werema asked to speak with me. I thought, "oh dear, I am being called out by the professor, in the first class…" But, Mr. Werema was simply curious. He told me he knew a lot about Moldova, including that it used to be part of the Soviet Union and gained independence. Then he said something that gave me a bit of confidence to get through my degree. He said, "don't feel intimidated by the rest of the students; trust me, you have something special they don't have, courage and perseverance. I see myself in you when I came to this country 20 years ago. I was a young guy from Kenya with little knowledge but a big dream, and look where I am today." I looked at him thinking, this guy doesn't know what he is talking about, he is a professor and I barely speak English. He followed up. "Miss Potinga, I bet you will finish top of your class." I stared back at him in shock and replied, "Mr. Werema, I pray I finish, period, I'm not even dreaming of being at the top of the class." He smiled. "Talk to me in 18 months, then we will see."

Lesson Learned: The power of someone believing in your abilities, even before you do.

Throw Your Running Shoes Off The Balcony

My job at American National was where my "real" career began. There I met my lifetime mentors, developed my Information Security skills, and, most importantly, learned more lessons on how to deal with adversity and obstacles in my path. One of my mentors and a big cheerleader for me at American National was Eric Davenport. Eric was Director of the Life Insurance division. He had recently relocated from a different office while his was being built, and he sat in a cubicle next to mine. Back then, I oversaw the life insurance policy reinstatement process, which was a time-sensitive and demanding task. I was trained by a real pro, Sharon, who had done the job for 20 years, so I knew the ins and outs of it comfortably.

One day, Sharon walked into my cubicle and asked how overwhelmed I was with an unusually large volume of reinstatement applications, and if I needed help to finish all of them in time. I told her not to worry; I had a plan on how to finish all of them in the next 48 hours. While I was describing my plan to her, Eric overheard our conversation, and after Sharon left he stopped by my cubicle to chit-chat.

He was very curious about how I had come up with such a plan. He asked me about my background and immigration story; he was genuinely intrigued. A couple of days later, he showed up with two books for me; one was *Monday Morning Leadership* by David Cottrell and the other *The Go-Getter* by Peter Kyne. I was floored by his kind gesture. He told me he saw a future leader in me, a go-getter. *The Go-Getter* is one of my all-time favorite books. There are more lessons contained in its few pages than there are in some novels. The story is about a man named Mr. William "Bill" Peck, a former soldier who is put through a test of obtaining a "blue vase" by his new employer. The author, Peter B. Kyne, details the story of how Cappy Ricks, the retired owner of Ricks Logging and Lumber Company, encourages the new President of the company, Mr. Skinner, to hire Bill Peck after discovering that he is a go-getter.

This book taught me some of the most valuable lessons of my life. First: **Believe in yourself**. The main character, Mr. Peck, offers a great reminder that we all need to believe in ourselves. If there is anyone who could consider themselves down and out, it is a war veteran with a bad limp and one and a half arms; but, Mr. Peck does not let this get him down. Second: **Act with determination**. Throughout the book, Mr. Peck displays his determination time and time again. From the beginning of the book when he was so determined to get the job that he already had business cards made, to later in the story when he refuses to take no for an answer and vows to do whatever it takes to obtain the "blue vase" for Cappy. And finally, the most important lesson: **Don't take "no" for an answer**. Time and time again, Mr. Peck reaches a point where it seems as if he is being told "no." He meets resistance in many situations in his pursuit of the "blue vase," but rather than packing it in and going home he finds ways to rethink his approach and create a new path towards it." This book is my favorite and I make it a habit to re-read it every year, each time gleaning new lessons from its pages.

Oftentimes in life, we need to be reminded to slow down and enjoy the fruits of our labor, to cherish the achievements we accomplish, however big or small. That was a bit of a problem for me back then. For instance, I was in my last semester of my master's, with wonderful grades and to my shocking surprise all "A's", I guess Mr. Werema knew what he was saying after all. Interestingly, I didn't actually set out to get all "A's", but because of my insecurities around not being good enough, I was studying and over studying just to make sure I kept up with the rest of the class.

We used to have team projects; in my team we had three other students, Karina, Lenny, and David. Karina was a mother working full-time and going to school. For Lenny, it was her second master's degree, and David worked in the medical field. All three of my teammates were brilliant people who I constantly had to work hard to keep up with. When I would write a paper or prepare my part of the project, I would cry and panic at the thought of being judged on my English proficiency. My poor roommate, Amanda, would read all of my papers just to help keep me calm. Eventually, I found out that all three of them thought my English wasn't too bad. In fact, they were the ones intimidated by me, being able to speak four languages fluently. Maybe it's a good thing I didn't know what they thought until the end – I might not have worked as hard to get the grades I did. But this experience makes me think about how much we fear what other people think about us. How we imagine we are being criticized and judged by other people when, in fact, it's quite possible it is the opposite. I realized in the end they were not criticizing me, I was. I was my own biggest critic.

Eric was my mentor during those challenging times, always there to cheer me up and give me words of wisdom. One day, I was sitting in his office talking about what would be next after I graduated. I had a list of things I wanted to do - what certifications I would get and the next thing I would learn. He was listening to me very carefully, until he interrupted me with an enlightening question. "When are you going to throw your running shoes off the balcony?" I was confused. "What are you talking about?" He chuckled and said, "when are you going to stop and celebrate these small victories in every stage of your journey?" I was still a little perplexed by his question. "I don't have time for any celebrations; I still have to grow personally and professionally!" Eric countered. "Celebrating little victories **is** beneficial for your growth." To which I replied, "I can't throw off my running shoes because, since I arrived in the U.S., I've felt like running and everyone else is walking. I am running to catch up with the rest of the crowd; I am running to keep up with the rest of the crowd."

Eric looked at me with a smile. "If you don't know when to stop and enjoy your little victories, what is the meaning of having victories?" It was an eye opener. I didn't know how to enjoy my little accomplishments. It was time to take a break from scrambling and begin enjoying the tasty little fruits of my labor.

Lesson Learned: Occasionally, don't forget to stop and enjoy the fruits of your labor.

Don't Take "No" For An Answer

For most people, the odds are invariably stacked against them the moment they decide to enter into a new adventure, or a new world. If they are to push past these barriers, they must learn the art of not accepting "no," because they will be told no every day, every week, every month, and every year. The moment they accept no will be the beginning of the end for them. For me, there is always a way and "no" simply isn't an answer. I come from a family of fighter, from my grandfather fighting in WWII to my father fighting the communist, socialist system and post-communist mafia. Whether fighting for life or for a brighter future, the fight never stopped in the Potinga family. We do not concede! As the great Winston Churchill said, "don't take 'no' for an answer, never submit to failure. Do not be fobbed off with mere personal success or acceptance. You will make all kinds of mistakes, but as long as you are generous and true, and also fierce, you cannot hurt the world or events." I do not give up easily. When I receive "no" as an answer, it doesn't stop me from pursuing my goal; rather, it motivates me to push even harder.

One of these situations presented itself to me a few months before graduating from TWU. I was selected for an international internship in London; the selection was made based on my grades and honor society membership. When I received the email from my school, I could hardly believe it - for a moment, I thought it was a scam. Here I am, almost finishing my graduate degree in the U.S. (one of my biggest dreams), and now I have been selected for an international internship? Unbelievable! I could not miss out on such an amazing opportunity. To be able to attend the internship, however, I had to request almost three months of unpaid leave from work, which was easier said than done.

American National has an old-school mentality when it comes to executives and their decision making. I had never heard of someone taking three months leave from one company to attend an internship at another, but that didn't stop me from raising the question to my department executives. First, I talked to Eric; he was beyond excited for me and told me not to give up, even if I encountered obstacles along the way. He told me to talk to our VP (follow the chain of command) so that the message would get to the right people. I did as I was told and spoke to my VP, explaining what a great opportunity it was for my future and requesting permission to take the three months leave. He promised to speak to our SVP and HR. Time was of the essence in my case, as I had to provide an answer to my school to get the paperwork in motion.

A week went by and I hadn't heard a word from my VP. I decided to ask Eric if he heard anything about my case; what he told me was both disappointing and encouraging at the same time. He revealed that my message didn't even make it out of our division; therefore, I should take matters into my own hands and reach out directly. So, since going through the chain of command didn't work, I went directly to the source who could provide me with an honest answer - the CEO of the company. Bold move I know, but I was not willing to give up on this opportunity easily. I told the his secretary that I needed 15 minutes with CEO to discuss an education matter. She was kind enough to put me on his schedule the next day. I knew well enough that one doesn't get a meeting with the CEO every day, so I needed to prepare and build my case.

I needed a strong case that would put me in a good light with the CEO in order for him to even entertain my request. I gathered my transcripts, all my certifications, and diplomas from the honor society to prove I was qualified to receive this internship. Once I got into his office, I was ready to pitch my case. He listened to me for a few minutes, and congratulated me on my achievements. Then he asked me if I had spoken to my immediate supervisor. I said I had, but unfortunately, my message wasn't transmitted through the chain of command, which is why I decided to go straight to the top. He liked me coming to approach him directly with the question, and he enjoyed seeing young people working hard for their future. "I wish we had more young people like you in our company. After all, we have an open-door policy, anyone can approach me," the CEO said. I was relieved; you never know how such an encounter can end up. He promised to speak to the President of HR about my request and have an answer by the following week, and he kept his word! Tuesday, I was contacted by the assistant to the HR president to schedule a meeting. I was nervous about what the outcome would be; again, I gathered all my accomplishments, practiced my speech, and prayed to God for a positive response. The HR president greeted me with a smile, which helped bolster my confidence and break the ice for conversation. He listened to me, looked at my documents, and then, to my surprise, said the following. "We are going to allow you to go experience this adventure. I am pleased to know that we have such young, talented people in our company. You could serve as an example for the entire company." I was speechless! I had tears in my eyes, tears of happiness and joy, upon hearing his response. Then, he added something even better. "Do you need any monetary support?" I replied. Well, Sir, I will be out of a job for three months, so any help would be very much appreciated." he smiled. "We will find a way to help you. We will ty to reimburse you for your master's degree." I was absolutely astonished by this generous offer – I felt I needed someone to pinch me, so I knew it was real. Me, a little girl originally from a country that no one has ever heard of, is getting the opportunity to travel to London for an internship!? How can that be possible? I was beyond excited, I never thought I would get such a chance when I first arrived in the U.S.; for a moment, I forgot this was the land of opportunity and that anything was possible.

All of these events were amazing, but there was still one, small problem – my immediate management. I was afraid of retribution from my department because I knew how they felt about my going around them to the CEO, but the HR president assured me that he would make sure there were no issues. He did talk to my management but they still held a grudge. Apparently, I had "overstepped my boundaries." From their perspective, I had wanted too much, reached too high. I was just "the little girl with an accent" who was not supposed to dream big. At one point, they called me into the office and tried to guilt me about leaving my coworkers strained for three months. When that didn't work, they tried to intimidate me by asking me to resign before I left. Finally, they pulled the immigration card to try and get me fired. My response? "Well, the CEO of this company, signed my request, and there is nothing you can do about it." Right then and there, I became public enemy number one I was persona non grata to my immediate management, and I knew there would be retaliation upon my return. I didn't care though; all I was focused on was enjoying my well-deserved internship and being grateful to the people who believed in me.

Lesson learned: The answer is always no until you ask again and again.

The Mentor

My summer in London was absolutely amazing. From the places I visited around the U.K. and Europe in my free time, to the experiences I gained working in a high end hotel as a global marketing assistant, it was easily one of the greatest adventures of my life. I met a lot of interesting people, some of whom became lifelong friends. After my summer in London finished, however, I had to return to the U.S. and it was a tough transition getting back into my old job and life after such an amazing time. However, I had given my word to the CEO and the HR president that I would return to my job no matter what, and I knew how important it was not to break that promise. So I returned as I said I would and, as expected, the retribution began almost immediately

My direct supervisor demoted me without stripping my title, from a manager I became a clerk. Then, he kicked me out of my original cubicle into a smaller one, just to hammer home that I was of little importance. I can be a very patient person though; I didn't react or give in to their manipulations. Nevertheless, everyone has their limit. The final straw was when my VP called me into his office to yell at me regarding my meeting with the CIO of the company. Despite the fact that the meeting was requested by CIO himself, my VP felt

I had again overstepped my boundaries. As I stood in his office explaining that the CIO arranged this meeting with the purpose of inquiring about my trip, he refused to accept my answer. He thought that the meeting was about my current situation in the department, and that somehow it could affect him directly. I was practically corned but something didn't allow me to just sit there and take his disrespectful comments. I took two steps toward his desk and said, "Sir, I don't know who you think you are, but you cannot talk to me in this manner. You are not acting as a leader but rather a bully, and I am not willing to stand here and listen to you be disrespectful towards me." As I finished my sentence, I slammed the door of his office and went to the restroom so no one could see me.

I was infuriated! So infuriated that I started crying. After a few minutes, I calmed down and went back to my desk to contemplate my next steps. What should I do next? Do I file a formal complaint? Do I tell the CEO and HR? What do I do? Right there, in that moment, my mom's words echoed through my mind, "be the bigger person." She always told me not to behave like the person who hurt or disrespected me, but to be the bigger person. Be the grown up in the room. After a day of thinking, I decided to talk to HR and ask for a transfer to a different department. I provided minimal details, but the HR representative was familiar with my situation and figured out the problem quickly.

A few days later I received a message from Richard Putz, CISO of the company. He scheduled a short meeting with me regarding a position available in the Information Technology Governance Risk and Compliance (GRC) department. I was ready to move, no matter what the position was. I had no idea what an important role Richard would play in my career. He met me with a smile, and we talked for 15 minutes about him and his family (who were from the same region as mine) and about me and my skills. By the end of our conversation, he offered me an analyst position with the GRC team. I was beyond grateful for the opportunity. Even though I had no idea what the role entailed, I was ready for the challenge. I mentioned I had no previous experience in the field, or even in IT, but he assured me I would do great. In two weeks, I was part of the Governance Risk and Compliance department. Everything was new to me; previously I was an accounting manager and now I was in a completely new, foreign field.

Luckily, challenges don't scare me, they inspire me. One advantage I had was having Richard by my side as my guide and mentor. Richard is an experienced professional with a diverse background, from a former Information Security and Cybersecurity consultant to CEO, CFO, and finally, CISO. His vast qualifications and experience guided me in this new journey. When you enter any new career, there are many doubts and questions. No matter what my new challenge was, either completing a project or studying for a new IT/Cybersecurity certification, Richard's comment was always the same. "You got this; I believe in you." His words were fuel to my fire. They gave me courage to conquer anything. I didn't really understand back then the value of such an amazing mentor. After I became more experienced and confident in the field, and got a few certifications under my belt, I looked back and realized what a tremendous influence he had on my development. Richard is a great mentor who is motivated and energized, cares about my growth, and is willing to commit his time. Even several years and companies later, I still reach out to him to discuss strategic choices in front of me, and get his sage wisdom on the world of cyber security and IT.

As Denzel Washington once said, "show me a successful individual and I'll show you someone who had real positive influences in his or her life. I don't care what you do for a living – if you do it well I'm sure there was someone cheering you on or showing the way. A mentor." For me it was and still is Richard. Having a mentor in your life is very valuable. I believe everyone needs at least one in their lifetime. They'll give you advice and inspiration that will completely change your trajectory. They'll also give you guidance and support should you stray from your potential. They'll even be a role model and guide whom you can follow.

Lesson Learned: Don't be afraid to get out of your comfort zone and try new things; but make sure you have a cheerleader by your side, a mentor.

The Divine Intervention

As you already know by now, I am a strong believer in a higher power and divine intervention. There are many circumstances in my life where God worked miracles to help me when I needed it most. There were times when I thought there was no way, no resolution, no positive outcome, and somehow out of nowhere a divine hand was extended to me for assistance. One of my favorite bible verses comes from 2 Corinthians 12:9: "My grace is sufficient for you, for my power is made perfect in weakness." I always felt God's grace and power, even in the most difficult and vulnerable moments of my life, his grace was ever present with me. One of these miracles was meeting my husband. Sometimes life is a circle, and you must complete it before you understand the meaning of the journey.

I previously mentioned that the first city I worked in after arriving in the U.S. was Corpus Christi, Texas. Eleven years before I met my husband, Christina rescued me when I needed it the most with a live-in job as babysitter for her kids, the eldest of whom was a little girl named Chloe. Fast forward eleven years and that little girl had just graduated high school, and her mother surprised her with a graduation party. An even bigger surprise was inviting her favorite nanny to celebrate! After a nice dinner, we decided to go to a bar for a few drinks. It was Sunday night and the bars in Corpus Christi were almost empty. We stopped by the one bar in Corpus that allowed 18-year-old entry, and when we got in there were about six people total, including us. While Christina, Chloe, our other two girlfriend, and I were enjoying a drink and chit-chatting near the bar, we heard a loud voice with a weird accent. "Hi girls, what are you celebrating tonight?" We turned around to be greeted with a 6'5" guy in cargo shorts and flip flops; he had a very weird but sexy accent. We figured the accent was South African or Australian, and after chatting a bit he confirmed he was Australian. What I noticed from the get-go was his manners; he was very respectful in his approach toward us with a gentlemanly demeanor. I was not looking for a date that night, I mean it was Sunday night in Corpus Christi after all. Yet, as we got talking, he mentioned he used to live in Houston but currently lives in Austin. I was surprised. "I live in Houston now, but I might be moving to Austin soon." We both stared at each other with a smile on our faces. Then, he looked at me and said," There will be 499 guys who would like to show you around Austin, can I be the one who actually does?" I thought, this guy is a bit cheesy but straightforward, I like that. I responded, "We will see by the end of the night." From further conversation it was clear he was a serious, responsible man with no time to play games. That was a relief to me, as I don't have time to waste or like to play games when it comes to relationships either. I decided to get into the nitty gritty <u>and</u> ask him a few serious questions. I asked him how old he was, why he was not married, and if he had any kids. His answer convinced me to give him my phone number and accept his proposal to go on a date in the future. He said, "I don't want to get married just for the sake of it. Marriage is a very important step in my life, and I want to be married forever. So I am still looking for the "one" to build a family with." It was an answer I had not heard from a man before. It was the answer of a mature and responsible man who knew what he wanted in life; it was rare. Not even a week later, he came to Houston to take me on a date and now we are married. The interesting thing was, I was interviewing for a job in Austin at that time and I was not sure I was going to get it. Well, never underestimate God's power; I got the job and we moved in together a month and half later. Let me tell you that we are a very rare couple - there are not many Moldovan-Australian couples out there but I love it! I enjoy our similarities and cherish our differences. Don't get me wrong, now and again there are some terminology/accent difficulties in our relationship, but I think it adds spice to our marriage and usually laughs (once the confusion has been cleared up).

My husband is a very considerate man. He knows that my family doesn't speak any English so he learned some Romanian, and for our wedding he even repeated his vows in Romanian so my parents could understand. Another amazing and shocking thing my husband did was ask my father for his permission to marry me. It was not the fact that he asked, it was the way he did it. We had been dating for almost two months when we took a short vacation to Moldova. First, we stopped in Germany where my brother lives and my dad works, temporarily. We were all sitting at the table eating, drinking, and having a good time. My now husband asked me to translate something to my father. It seemed like a normal request; I was translating the entire night after all. He says, "Tell your dad I love your daughter, would you allow me to marry her?" I didn't finish translating the sentence as I was so shocked by his question! I had no idea he was going to ask my dad to marry me and to ask me to translate it for him! My dad was confused too, as I had only translated half of the sentence to him. With tears in my eyes, I finished translating. He was beyond happy for us, and of course gave his blessing to my now husband to marry his daughter.

Both my husband and I believe that it was God's intervention and plan for us to meet, fall in love, and get married. He was in Corpus Christi for the first time, for one afternoon, to meet a mate of his he had randomly met in Houston a couple years earlier, only to meet me that evening. I had to wait eleven years and go back to where everything started to meet my future husband. How crazy is that? But God had a beautiful plan for both of us, and we are very grateful and blessed for such a miracle.

Lesson Learned: God will always intervene when you need Him most!

Becoming An "American"

Have you ever asked yourself what it means to be an American? Or even better, what it takes to become an American? What makes an American? How does it feel to belong to this nation? These questions might sound absurd to some, but certainly not to an immigrant. I have asked them to myself countless times before becoming an American citizen in 2018; and for every single person the idea means something different. I always felt blessed to be able to immigrate to America; in fact, I consider myself one of the luckiest people alive. Many people in the world can only dare to dream of immigrating to this

Promised Land and living the American experiment. Only in America can a person who has nothing become someone who has it all. However, I didn't fully understand what it takes to be a true American until I went through the citizenship process and attended the ceremony. It is not exactly a cakewalk; yet, it's much less complex than other countries (i.e. Switzerland, Israel, Australia). Before I had my final interview with the immigration agent, I received a guide with questions and answers about the United States' systems of civics and government, as well as U.S. history. To be able to pass my test, I had to study 100 questions about all three subjects. While I was going through the questions, I began to fully realize what it means to be an American. The civic, governmental, and historical questions painted a perfect picture as to why America is and continues to be the greatest country in the world. It was founded on the values of liberty, freedom, and opportunity, and that isn't something to scoff at. The Constitution and the Bill of Rights, together with the additional amendments, are some of the greatest documents to have ever been written.

Are they perfect? No, but very little in this world is. Trust me when I tell you though that there are a lot of places in the world where all of these freedoms and opportunities are not automatically granted, or worse, prohibited. The Constitution is great not only because of what is written in it, but because it is more than just a document – it is the heartbeat of America. It's a symbol of equality, liberty, opportunity, and happiness – the qualities Americans value the most. Without this document, America would not be the land of opportunity the world flocks to enjoy. I have never met George Washington, James Madison, or Abraham Lincoln, however, what brought me to America was their American dream and the promise of a better life for me and my progeny.

Just to give you a better understanding of how many people around the world want to become American citizens, I will describe my swearing in ceremony. At the ceremony there were 3,540 people from 178 countries receiving their U.S. citizenship. That's pretty impressive, considering there are 195 countries in the world and the ceremony is held once every month. Can you imagine how many people become U.S. citizens on an annual basis? If this country did not offer the opportunities, it does, the demand would not be so high. People strive to come to this wonderful country, to become part of such a great nation, as I did thirteen years ago. The most important part of the citizenship ceremony is the Oath of Allegiance. By taking the Oath of Allegiance, you swear to support the principles of the United States Constitution and defend its values. Only after taking the oath does one become a U.S. citizen. This moment was very touching and important to me because the Constitution contains the rights and responsibilities all U.S. citizens shoulder. You can't have one without the other; it's a package deal. You take the oath voluntarily, no one forces you to do so. Being aware of the importance of such an oath is imperative.

My husband and I are very grateful to be part of this nation where we met and created a family. One of our biggest goals is to teach our children to values this country and to be proud of being an American. We want them to grasp the fact that being born and raised on American soil, especially in Texas, is a privilege and a blessing. We hope they will understand that this land was touched by God's grace and they should never take it for granted.

America - The Architect of My Destiny

I truly believe anyone who has lost their sense of what it means to be an American or is ungrateful to be a part of such a great nation should go and review the citizenship process. The oath taken serves as a good reminder of why this nation has endured over the centuries – why it is standing tall and proud because it learned from its mistakes and grew stronger from them, instead of giving in and failing as other nations have. No matter how you feel politically, there's always room for national pride. This doesn't mean ignoring the issues. It's important to stand up for what you believe in. The distinction is, here, you have the explicit right and freedom to do just that. But, I think it only works when we also honor and celebrate our country's accomplishments. After all, many people fought and died for the lives we lead in America today. Please, DO NOT take your freedom for granted!

Lesson Learned: America, thank you for giving me the opportunity to be part of one of the greatest nations on earth.

FOOTNOTES

1. D'Souza, D. (2020). United States of socialism: Who's behind it. Why it's evil. How to stop it. New York, NY: All Points Books, an imprint of St. Martin's Publishing Group.
2. Skolnick, E. J. (2012). Raising Your Game: Over 100 Accomplished Athletes Help You Guide Your Girls and Boys Through Sports. iUniverse.
3. Covey, S. R. (2013). The 7 Habits Of Highly Effective People (India Only ed.). SIMON & SCHUSTER.
4. Brown, B. (2010). The Gifts of Imperfection: Let Go of Who You Think You're Supposed to Be and Embrace Who You Are (1st ed.). Hazelden Publishing.
5. Collins, J. (2001). Good to Great: Why Some Companies Make the Leap and Others Don't (1st ed.). HarperBusiness.
6. Byrne, R. (2006). The Secret (10th Anniversary ed.). Atria Books/Beyond Words.
7. Saad, G. (2020). The Parasitic Mind: How Infectious Ideas Are Killing Common Sense. Regnery Publishing.
8. Kyne, P. B. (2013). The Go-Getter: A Story That Tells You How To Be One. CreateSpace Independent Publishing Platform.

9. Whewell, B. T. (2015, June 18). The great Moldovan bank robbery. BBC News. https://www.bbc.com/news/magazine-33166383
10. A Href=/Team/Lucia-Casap Hreflang=En>Lucia CasapWhy students in Moldova are performing better. World Bank Blogs. https://blogs.worldbank.org/education/why-students-moldova-are-performing-better
11. Jandl, M. (2017, March 2). Moldova Seeks Stability Amid Mass Emigration. Migrationpolicy.Org. https://www.migrationpolicy.org/article/moldova-seeks-stability-amid-mass-emigration
12. O'Neill, L. (2009, April 21). The World's Most Unhappy People. WSJ. https://www.wsj.com/articles/SB124025997653636315
13. Karlsson, P. A. B. (2019, July 26). Moldova, A Wine Experience Out Of The Ordinary. Forbes. https://www.forbes.com/sites/karlsson/2019/07/25/moldova-a-wine-experience-out-of-the-ordinary/#1dff9a555b05
14. Notable & Quotable: Milton Friedman. (2015, June 14). WSJ. https://www.wsj.com/articles/notable-quotable-milton-friedman-1434318595
15. Zacharias, R. (2004). Can Man Live Without God (unknown ed.). Thomas Nelson.

Bio

Majority of people acknowledge the importance of sharing their life journey - each of us has a special place in the world and the experience we had can never be repeated or replaced. Writing a memoir is overwhelming but rewarding at the same time.

Tatiana Potinga Merry was born and raised in Chisinau, Moldova; and she fluently speaks 4 languages, Romanian, Russian, English, and Spanish. She went to primary school in Moldova and got her first degree there as well. Afterwards, in 2008 she moved to the United States where she received an MBA from Texas Woman's University. She has had the chance to live and work abroad, most notably in the United Kingdom. After performing an internship in London, UK in 2015, she returned to the US. Tatiana currently resides with her family in Austin, Texas working in the Information Security and Cyber Security field.

www.ingramcontent.com/pod-product-compliance
Lightning Source LLC
Chambersburg PA
CBHW071217160426
43196CB00012B/2330